Lock Picking

The Complete Guide for Beginners to Master

(Learn How to Open Locked Doors Yourself with Ease)

Kevin Landes

Published By **Chris David**

Kevin Landes

All Rights Reserved

Lock Picking: The Complete Guide for Beginners to Master (Learn How to Open Locked Doors Yourself with Ease)

ISBN   978-1-7779885-9-3

No part of this guidebook shall be reproduced in any form without permission in writing from the publisher except in the case of brief quotations embodied in critical articles or reviews.

Legal & Disclaimer

The information contained in this book is not designed to replace or take the place of any form of medicine or professional medical advice. The information in this book has been provided for educational & entertainment purposes only.

The information contained in this book has been compiled from sources deemed reliable, and it is accurate to the best of the Author's knowledge; however, the Author cannot guarantee its accuracy and validity and cannot be held liable for any errors or omissions. Changes are periodically made to this book. You must consult your doctor or get professional medical advice before using any of the suggested remedies, techniques, or information in this book.

Upon using the information contained in this book, you agree to hold harmless the Author from and against any damages, costs, and expenses, including any legal fees potentially resulting from the application of any of the information provided by this guide. This disclaimer applies to any damages or injury caused by the use and application, whether directly or indirectly, of any advice or information presented, whether for breach of contract, tort, negligence, personal injury, criminal intent, or under any other cause of action.

You agree to accept all risks of using the information presented inside this book. You need to consult a professional medical practitioner in order to ensure you are both able and healthy enough to participate in this program.

Table Of Contents

Chapter 1: The Underside Of Lock & Key . 1

Chapter 2: Various Lock Models 11

Chapter 3: Set-Up & Practice 17

Chapter 4: Scrubbing 22

Chapter 5: Exercises 26

Chapter 6: Master Lock Picking 37

Chapter 7: Lock Characteristics 42

Chapter 8: Tools 57

Chapter 9: Mechanisms 63

Chapter 10: Lever Lock 69

Chapter 11: Warded 80

Chapter 12: Pin Tumbler As Well As Wafer
.... 88

Chapter 13: Bicycle Chain 104

Chapter 14: Mechanisms 107

Chapter 15: Lever Lock 114

Chapter 16: Pin Tumbler & Wafer 128

Chapter 17: Padlocks 141

Chapter 18: A Quick Background Of Locks And Lock Picking 153

Chapter 19: Different Locks And Mechanisms.. 157

Chapter 20: Tools And Equipment Of The Locksmith.. 163

Chapter 21: Make Your Own Lock Picks As Well As Tension Wrenches................... 168

Chapter 22: Different Methods For Unlocking Locked Doors....................... 174

Chapter 1: The Underside Of Lock & Key

So how do you open the door of a lock? This is the question we'll tackle within this chapter.

The language used for the primary elements of a lock differs from one manufacturer to another and even between locations The best way to determine this is by referring to the following diagram if you're experiencing any confusion in the labeling of the manufacturer as well as the descriptions in this chapter.

A Basic Cylindrical Lock (Pin Tumbler Lock)

The pin tumbler lock (a cylindrical lock) for a discussion of the lock's internal workings and method by which a key can open the lock. Further on in the chapter, we'll look at how picking may alter the inner workings of the lock.

(not an image that has been approved; graphic department reference]

A cylindrical lock typically utilized by deadbolts or pin tumbler lock. When the cylindrical (the plug) of a pin tumbler lock gets rotated by the key, the cam attached is pulled in by the bolt and opens the door. In the same way, if the plug or cylinder is rotated the opposite way it releases the bolt by the cam. This snaps into a spring, locking the bolt in it's place. Deadbolt locks only have the cylinder that can slide the bolt in a circular motion and not the spring thus making it more secure. The latch driven by a spring is simpler to control.

The diagram above illustrates the keyway for the plug. Keyways function as an intricate puzzle to find the key. Keys are placed in the keyway. It is a ward-shaped protrusion which interact with the key. They limit what keys can unlock the lock. If the right key is put in, the plug spins while the hull is not.

A cylindrical lock there are a number of paired pins. Each pair is positioned inside a shaft that is located in the plug's central area up into the housing of the plug. They are set with springs located on uppermost point on the shafts. When no key has been in the lock, then each pair's bottom pin is within the plug. The top pin extends about halfway out of the housing as well as halfway away to the plug, ensuring that the plug won't rotate and is securely anchored in the lock housing.

The keys' notches push the pins up to specific degrees when the key is put into the lock. When you insert a incorrect key, the pins on top will be placed partially inside the housing, and partly within the plug, and the plug in the lock won't move and the door may not be opened.

"Pin one" is the first pin that the key comes in contact with and is followed by the next pin, the third, fourth, and fifth (depending on the number of pins are in the lock). Every pin is raised by the key until the gap between driver pin as well as the key pin ends when it reaches the line of shear. After all pins are at that line, then the plug spins to open the lock. The pins' connector points must be with the shear line directly because it's that part of the lock that the housing and the cylinder meet. The pins should be located in the opposite direction of the shear line, with they must be within the plug, while the higher pins are within the home - otherwise the lock won't fully open. If you use the wrong key then any of the pins might not get to the shear line, instead they might protrude between the hull and the plug which can block the rotation that the plug is able to make. When the correct key is used the pins will not be attaching the plug to the housing. Therefore, it is able to rotate, pushing the bolt out, or bringing it in.

So, a lock works for people that don't understand the mechanism it operates and how you can manipulate it. Now that you've mastered the essential parts of a lock and keys, knowing how to select it ought to be simple the only thing you need to do is line these pins in a shear line. It is crucial to be aware that pins can differ for pin tumblers which makes certain locks more difficult to identify in comparison to others. As an example, many pin tumblers feature top pins with mushroom-shaped heads. If you try to pull the pin on top upwards, the shape of the mushroom could cause the pin to slide before you've had a chance to get the pin clear. This could be a problem as you try to establish familiar with the inner functioning of the lock and particularly, when putting the pins. Be aware of this when training.

How to Pick a Pin Tumbler Lock

In the case of a pin tumbler lock keys simply place the pins to align in a shear line. that's what you'll need to accomplish using your torque wrench and choose - aligning each pair of pins to the proper place. This is not done in a single step however, only one pin at a.

What exactly is the term torque wrench? A torque wrench can be described as a tool which can be inserted in the keyhole, and then turn to offset the plug slightly away from the housing of the lock. It's an easy tool available in a variety of sizes, however it is in its most basic design, a thin flat-head screwdriver.

What about a pick? The picks have to extend inside the lock before pressing the pins upwards, which is why they're usually thin pieces made of metal that are with a curving curve towards one end.

The pin tumbler lock with just four steps. While the idea is straightforward but the actual procedure may be more challenging to learn. First, let's discuss the theory.

Step 1: Insert Torque Wrench & Turn

The first step is to turn the torque wrench into the key hole the way that you would turn an e-key. In the same way, it is going to offset the plug and the housing. This will create within the shafts of pins small gaps into which you could insert your wrench and raise the pins.

Step 2: Insert Your Pick & Maneuver First Pin Pair

While inserting your pick it is important to lift every pair of pins up until the top pin has been shifted to the full extent of the housing like a right key does. Use a gentle pressure using the torque wrench, and then follow the direction of your finger. When you've pressed the pin in the right place, you'll sense or hear the sound of the pin moving onto the shaft's ledge that's what keeps the pin's upper part inside its housing. If it was not held to the ledge, it could slide into the hole.

Step 3: Push each pin pair into place

Make your way through every pin pair and then move them on the shear lines, using each pin on top being pressed into the housing as well as each of the lower pins pressing in the socket.

Step 4: Open the Lock

Similar to the correct key, when all pin pairs have been aligned with the line of shear, then the plug can rotate and open the lock.

Technique

You can see that it's a simple task However, mastering the process is the most difficult aspect. Through repetition, exactly the quantity of pressure you need to apply and be able to detect the distinctive clicking of the pins dropping to the floor. When you practice, you should be able to see the components of the lock, as well as its layout. In addition, your sense of force should be sharpened to be able to sense even the smallest movement of the plugs and pins.

Another technique is known as "raking." Locksmiths often begin with this method that is quicker and more precise than picking. This technique requires you to force the wide-tip pick towards the inside on the plug. Then, you pull the pick away quickly, with the intention to bump the pins while it's pulled out. In the meantime with the torque wrench rotate the plug to ensure that the pins on top be able to fall onto the edge of the rotating plug. If none of the pins are secured, attempt raking the lock another time or select the remaining pins by hand.

This is our first look at an ordinary cylindrical lock. Now we'll look at various lock designs to discover how their mechanical and internal components differ. You need to alter the style you use to pick and method accordingly.

Chapter 2: Various Lock Models

Flatland Model

Like similar to the circular lock (or the majority of locks to be precise) The flatland lock lets you use the right key to unlock the lock by aligning two the metal parts. In this instance, two pieces of steel are placed on top of each other and holes are made through the two plates. This creates an asymmetric lock, in which pins are placed. The gap between the two plates isn't in line with the gap between the "key pin" (on the side)) as well as"driver pin" (on the top) "driver pin" (on the top). The lower plate is surrounded by an extension beneath it that helps keep the pins on the top plate, and the driver pin is held down with a spring on that of the upper plate. The plates do not slide over them, as driver pins travel between the two plates. Like any lock or key, the key that is right can raise the pins and align them with the line of shear.

Another key feature of flatland locks is that the allowance for sliding between the top and bottom plates allows for a variety of keys are able to unlock the lock. Also, the lock is simpler to select, because there is no need to place the pins in a precise way like other locks like in the third illustration.

Wafer-Tumbler

The lock with a wafer-tumbler is a different form of cylindrical lock similar to that of the pin tumbler. Instead of pins but it comes with round tumblers that are shaped like wafers. Because the keyholes are typically larger in locks that have wafers and the tumblers are more easy to select than pins in a pin tumbler. These locks can be present in a lot of locking cabinets, filing cabinets and automobiles and are also found in numerous padlock styles.

The design of your lock with a wafer tumbler The wafers could be in pairs or singles and they're filled by a spring that is linked to the lock's housing and extended out of the cylindrical. When the key is correct that is used, the wafers are pushed down, and then pulled back to the plug precisely at the right spot. When the wrong key is used or the wrong key, the wafers could get pulled too low or insufficiently, meaning the plug won't be able to slide.

If you encounter the double-wafer locking, you'll need to utilize your torque wrench to exert pressure and then work the two wafers at both ends of the plug.

Tubular Locks

Often, they are more costly than wafer tumbler or pin tumbler locks for security, you'll get a greater value for money by using a tubular lock since it's more intricate and hard to identify. The cylinder's plug is made up of not just only a single row of pins rather, the entire length. The lock picking strategy isn't often successful with a tubular lock.

Pin Column Lock

These models have multiple pins, while a pin column locks is a pin lock with a single pin which could indicate the relationship between the torque that is applied as well as the force needed for lifting the pin. It is believed that the "feel" of picking depends upon this connection. Being a professional lockpicker, being aware of the way a pin can be manipulated through the force of your finger and the torque of the wrench can be key...no no pun meant.

The pin's movement from its position in the beginning is directly dependent on the amount of pressure needed for it to be moved. In the pin-column model there exist three forces that act on the driver pin: the force of spring emanating from the top of the pin the friction on the sides of the pin and the forces from the key pin that is below. If the pins are pressurized to the inside of the hull force from spring is increased. The pins move when you apply the correct quantity of pressure in order to counter the force generated by spring. When you apply torque friction causes pressure between the driver's pin as well as the plug hole. This makes the pins less able to move. but, you must apply pressure in order to combat the tension and spring force to get the pins be aligned. The right amount of pressure will allow the top of the driver pins to line up with the shear line permitting the plug to move.

If the lock is of a different kind, a second pin is then used to bind the lock. While the friction created by the pin that was first used has been eliminated but the force from springs persists, as is the second force, which is caused by the pin that is for key rubbing on the inside of the hull. To move to the next pin it is necessary increase the pressure. However, a pin column lock only has one pin. So when you've applied enough force to get the pin aligned with the line of shear, it's jiggered the lock and let the pin to move.

Chapter 3: Set-Up & Practice

Before we dive deeper into the specifics of the lock's characteristics, we'll learn a few practical skills under your toes. It's first time create your workstation. The collection of the tools you'll require will allow you to envision what you'll need to do and the workings of the various types of locks.

Assemble Your Tools

Torque Wrench

There is no need for the lock pick set rather, substitute the torque wrench by using the Allen wrench, a newspaper clip, or screwdriver. When using the Allen wrench, one could utilize a grinder or file to reduce the wrench to dimensions - it should be able to fit into the keyway. The size should be reduced until it will fit into the keyway. No less, not more. Also, you can make use of a strong paper clip. It is necessary to straighten it and make a loop at the one end that is that is large enough to slip through the key-way. The remaining wire needs to be bent approximately 90 degrees towards the end of the loop. A screwdriver of a small size could also be utilized However, ensure that the size is sufficient to reach the opposite side, since you'll require to move it around with sufficient force.

Pick

When you're picking the initial pin, employ any of the tools however, when you move to the next one it will be necessary to change the pin you select. We shouldn't be too quick to judge. The Allen wrench, paper clip, screw driver and a safety pin a straight pin or even a staple could serve as picks. If you're employing a Allen wrench or a screw driver, it is recommended to select the most compact one that is you can find. A staple or paper clip is required to be durable enough to take the force of springs and be straightened to be flat. Straight or safety pin must have its point removed so that you do not get yourself stung.

Purchase a Lock

Find a lock you want to test on. One that can aid you in identifying its components. It is possible to harm the lock as a result of working with it, therefore make sure you don't invest too much on it. Likewise, you shouldn't make use of it if you wish to get it to be able to work. Start by using a deadbolt 5 pin tumbler (most deadbolts have this model) that you could buy at any department shop. Be careful not to buy a cheap lock because inexpensive locks tend to be hard to open, even if you have keys. An ordinary or Kwikset deadbolt lock can be simpler to take apart.

Remove All Pins Except One

Don't forget, you're just a beginner Don't go the way of your own head. Making a decision on a five-pin tumbler is a skill you'll learn in the future But first, you'll begin by selecting just one of the pins. This way you'll get a feel of making a good choice, since it's a challenge initially to gain the sense of the process. Be careful not to damage the lock when taking out the pins. Make sure you leave the pin nearest to the lock's entrance order for you to watch the process unfold while you work.

Pick Your First Pin

Learn what you've learned thus far in this guide and apply it to your own life. Try working on the lock turned upside down since it's often more straightforward. Use your torque wrench to push slightly into the lock and then put in the pick while slowly lowering the pin that you're working on. It will be evident when you have nailed the shear line because the plug turns. There you are. the line. It is possible to practice it repeatedly using the same plug by returning it in its locked position before taking it out again.

Attempt Multiple Pins

It's easy to feel this now. Now you could add another pin to the mix. It's just behind the pin you've already got. Be careful not to overdo it and practice little by little to get better at it. It could take several days to master the 5-pin pick as well as an extensive set of equipment to accomplish this. It is likely that you will be able to select three pins using the common tools mentioned earlier, however If you're looking to go to the next level, it is recommended to purchase a pick set to practice an experience with it.

Chapter 4: Scrubbing

Different models that we've reviewed show the flaws that exist in locks. These allow an average locksmith, or lockpick fanatic to alter their locks. When you lift the pins each one at a time You don't require a tool or key to unlock your standard lock. All you require is some patience and repetition.

Although practicing at home comes with limited time however, when you're stuck and time is of most crucial importance. In this chapter on how you can improve the speed of scrubbing using a method known as scrubber.

Scrubbing occurs when the right quantity of pressure is applied when you move the pick over the pins in all directions, enough to eliminate spring and friction forces however, it is less than the collision force that results from the pin that is colliding with the hull. This technique typically requires the lockpicker to be trained enough to be able to feeling for the correct pressure and torque. If you can masterfully apply these steps as your pick passes across a pin, the Pin will rise and strike the hull, but will not go through it. It will cause the plug to turn, which is able to catch the driver pin along the edges of the plug just above the shear lines. By using just one stroke of your pick between the pins, your lock will be opened. This is only applicable to people who are a pro at scrubber. But even then, the majority often, just two or three pins are get set after the initial scrub, and a few more might be required, with adjustments in the amount of torque that you're applying for the pin.

The method is simple, as instead of being focused on the pins individually, you're needing to establish the right tension and torque. If the lock doesn't allow opening using this method then you'll need be able to open it one pin at a time. pin. There is a chance that you will see a lock's pins will be set in a particular order this is typically caused by an inconsistency between the axes of the drill holes and the plug's center line. This means that the pins move from back to front when turned in one direction while the reverse happens if it is reversed according to the tilt of the pin holes as well as the center line.

Here are step-by-step directions to help you master this speedier and more effective technique.

Step 1: Test Your Lock

Put in the torque wrench and select. Before applying the force, feel the force of the springs in the lock by taking the pick away.

Step 2: Apply Some Torque

Use a moderate quantity of torque before inserting the pick, taking care not to come in contact with pins. Then, you can quickly pull the pick away with enough force to counteract the force of spring however, not excessively.

Step 3: Increase Torque

After each wash, apply more force until the pins are become fixed. Driver pins should be able to catch onto the plug.

Step 4: Scrub

Continue to maintain your torque, and then scrub through the pins that are yet to be set. If the pins do not appear to get set, reduce your torque.

Chapter 5: Exercises

After you've had a go at the process of scrubbing and picking now is the time to refine your techniques. Because practice is essential for unlock picking and scrubbing, these exercises will assist you in mastering the art of picking. Instead of being focused on your final outcome that you can open the lock, concentrate on improving your technique while working through these exercises. By doing this, you will be able to increase your skills and get a better feel for the lock, without getting exhausted and throwing in the towel. Do it in short, intense bursts over 30 minutes or less Otherwise, your hands as well as your mind are likely to be tight, tense and unsuitable to gaining proficiency in locking picking.

Exercise 1: Getting a Feel for Torque

The most common error made by novice pickers is using excessive or consistent quantities of torque without altering the torque level. The range of torque needed to unlock the lock. It is essential to match the quantity of torque to the force of the pick as well as with additional forces at play within the lock.

It is necessary to apply only the smallest amount of force in order to stop the friction created by the plug's movement inside the hull. Place your torque wrench in the plug and record the quantity of torque needed to turn the plug around before the pins are bound. Certain locks will require more torque in comparison to others, like ones that have damaged water due to snow or rain. In the case of padlocks, the amount of torque needed should be accounted for by the force of the spring and the connection between the shackle bolt with the plug.

The highest level of tension can be measured through using the pick's flat surface to force all pins to the ground, then once you have removed the pick trying to apply the force of a large amount so that those pins remain in place. It should lead to the crucial pins being driven deeply into the hull which is where torque will hold it, and the pressure and torque will be too high. The test of this max torque can allow you to determine the exact amount of torque you should use - the range is between the minimum value checked by rotating the plug, and the highest quantity tested.

The scrubbing method can also assist you in determining the amount of torque needed. Then, apply increasing torque slowly while applying your choice of pins until you see some pins have set. Some pins become harder to push down, and eventually they will cease to be springy altogether. When you reach the point where you can maintain the torque level and then scrub the pins a few additional times by using the tool until they are set.

The ability to feel the torque is vital to be able in lock-picking make sure you practice until feel comfortable using it.

Exercise 2: Getting a Feel for Pick Pressure

Like torque, you need to apply the pressure that your pick receives. At first, you should only apply pressure to your pick when taking the pick out of the lock. When you've mastered that it's time to pressurize the pick during your pick's insertion too.

Utilizing your pick and torque wrench inside the lock, pull the pin on the front of the lock using the flat edge of your pick but without applying any force. The pressure you apply should only counter the force generated by springs, allowing you to gauge how much pressure that you apply. If you press on the pin down, the force increases, so check to determine the amount of pressure necessary to force all pins downwards when you remove the pick out of the lock. When the pick is removed it will cause the pins to come back into action, generating the noise. Take a look at each pin using your finger - they'll rise as you press the pins down. They will burst when the pick moves past them. This is the smallest amount of amount of pressure that your pick needs to exert on them.

To determine the highest pressure apply all lock pins in a single at a time, using the flat side of the pick. One pin could need the same amount of pressure according to the spring's stiffness. The new locks could have stiffer springs. Therefore, the increase in pressure on the pick is vital.

Exercise 3 Practice applying Fixed Pick Pressure Knowing how to bounce your pick will assist you in mastering the application of the fixed pressure applied to your pick while it moves within the lock. Every pin will have a different resistance. Therefore, the pressure applied to them by the pick should bounce in accordance with the resistance. Do not focus too much on the movement of the handle of your pick. Focus only the tip of the pick, since this is the primary aspect of choosing.

The manner in which the pick is held influences the way the pressure is put on. Make sure that you hold your pick in a way in a way that the pressure is able to be applied beyond your fingers or wrists and not from your shoulders or elbows. If you are scrubbing the lock, be aware of which finger joints are being used as well as those which are fixed. Joints used for the scrub need to be able and flexible enough to handle the pressure.

Try holding your pick using three fingers. One to lift the pick and allow pressure to be applied, and another for an angle for the pick. You can also keep your pick in the same way as pencils using the pressure applied via your wrist and movement provided through your shoulder and elbow. The wrist is not employed for movement only, but also pressure application.

Another option is to apply the scrubbing technique in order to gain a feel for the bounce of the pick within the keyway. You must ensure that your lock is opened in order to prevent the pins from push down. So the pick is able to scrub through the pins' different sizes, and rattle while it scrubs across them. The sound and the feel can be heard when the pin is set precisely. Although a pin might appear as if it's been in place, but there is no rattle it is actually incorrectly set, which means you be required to rectify this by disabling torque until they return to the original place or press them further.

Exercise 4: Determining Which Pins are Set

It is the ability to recognize the pins that are fixed is the main aspect of choosing locks. If you are practicing, be sure to keep an eye in the recognition of the pins set. It will be easy to identify them pins, since the pin will exhibit a little give. you can apply a only a little pressure. After that, it will cease to move. When you take off the tiny pressure that was applied to the pin, it is likely to rebound. Also, you will be able to know when an item is set by flicking it by hand and hearing their rattling. The sound of rattling will help you distinguish pins that are set as opposed to falsely set or unset ones.

If you're trying to figure out which side of the lock, the pins are placed - either the rear or front - it is possible to run your finger through the pins and hear these distinct elements. Repeat this process using the plug that is turned in the reverse direction. If the back pins are have been set using the plug turning in towards one direction forward, the front pins be set when the plug is in the opposite direction in the opposite direction; and vice versa.

If you're not sure the number of pins placed, you can remove the tension and observe how many clicks you hear. These sounds are caused by pins return to their position. The sounds will vary when pins snap back or when only one pin snaps back. False pins can too snap back. Recognizing the amount of snaps or clicks allows you to figure out how many pins have to be set.

Repeat this practice by applying different pressures and torque. The more torque used, the greater pressure is required to align the pins. When you have a large amount in pressure, the pins are likely to become stuck inside the hull and inaccessible.

Exercise 5: Visualization

As you work through these tasks, visualizing the steps you're doing is crucial in understanding the functioning that the lock operates. For the purpose of visualizing when you've open a lock, it is important to recollect before you mind the physical procedure and the connections that you've made as part of your analysis of the pins' setting. Instead of being content with your results, consider thinking about the steps you took as well as what transpired inside the lock, so you're able to make improvements on the next time you try.

Your visual skills need to be improved towards mastering lock picking take the time to practice your skills by picking a lock that is simple that is easy to pick. Remember the sensational and visual procedure of picking the lock. Then, go over the process step-bystep through your head, taking note of both the force and torque application, the strength of the lock as well as the sensation of the pins' position. Once you've got the image clear in your head then try to pick the lock once more using the same thought pattern that guides your movements. This will enable you to control your pressure as well as the muscles in your body, as well as let you evaluate the senses of your body, including touching and hearing. The visualization of the entire process and the locking's components can help you improve your pick-up skills and provide you with a base that will allow you to identify what's happening inside the lock as well as the actions necessary to get it open.

Chapter 6: Master Lock Picking

When you're proficient with basic locking picking, moving on to mastering lock picking implies that you have to refine your skills, including analytical thinking and visualisation. These are the qualities that distinguish people who picks according to their own speed and one who is able to pick at the speed and flexibility that emergency situations require.

Mechanics

The mechanics behind picking and particularly of scrubbing aren't as simple than one might imagine. The skills in mechanical dexterity and mechanics gained in childhood demand one to keep their hands in a specific position independent of the force. In addition, as it is necessary to put a fixed force to the pins each time you take the pick out of the lock, locking picking involves the use of a constant force, that is independent of your hands' positions. The pick must let the pick bounce around in the keyway, and in direct reaction to the pin's resistance.

In order to improve your skills in mechanical take note of the sensation and the sound produced by your movements between your pick and pins. As you repetition, you'll develop the understanding that's necessary in order to progress from the basic advanced locking picking.

Analytical Thinking

The locks are different, and so do the issues to pick the right one. But, the ability to recognize and utilize specific characteristics of particular types or models of locks makes the rest of the procedure much easier. This is where analytic thinking can be a huge help. In order to improve your pick it is necessary to know the characteristics of a lock by studying the signals transmitted to your fingertips when you manipulate the lock. The more you are familiar with the features of different locks, the more easy you will be able to analyse your choices and adjust your method.

Imagine your tools as functional and insightful. While you drag your pick over the pins it will gather data regarding the lock. The analysis is then used to modify the force of the torque wrench. This can set the pins to the shear line, and then open the lock. In the case of a lock, for instance, you find out in your research that the middle pins have been put in position, but the pins at the ends aren't yet been set, whenever you place the pick between those pins in the middle, make sure you boost the torque to ensure that the pins set are not loosened during the process. Also, you can lower the amount of torque if you think that one pin isn't rising enough as the pick passes over it. Variation in torque is essential to setting every pin in its place and the procedure of finding the right amount of torque is just more of an analytical process as it is physical, that requires precise coordination, and greater precision in analysis.

Visualization

Like we mentioned in the previous section about basic lock picks, visualization can aid you to open the lock at the time It will also allow you review and evaluate your actions. By absorbing the sensory information of your eyes, hands and ears, you will be able to make connections between your thoughts regarding the inner workings of the lock as well as your movements. The hands and your ears will inform you of the moment a pin is placed while your eyes assist you in coordinating your actions, particularly in the initial stages of. The combination of all your senses assist in visualizing and result your concentration with a level which is relaxed and focused. This will help you make the right steps to unlock the lock.

Chapter 7: Lock Characteristics

In order to improve your skills for advanced skills, you must be aware of the different features of various locks. The range of features is the one that determines your method of dealing with every lock. The locks that can't be removed usually include one or more the features listed below. We can help you identify the characteristics of your lock and then employ the correct techniques to deal with those characteristics.

The Direction of the Plug's Rotation

If you decide to pick locks, make sure you first determine which direction the plug turns, or else you'll be wasting long hours and energy without any result. The mechanism for the bolt decides which direction the plug will turn. It is possible to determine the proper direction of rotation by rotating the plug, and then observing whether it is able to rotate freely until it ceases to rotate. That is not the correct way. If you rotate the plug in the correct direction you'll feel resistance as the spring in the bolt and cam are in contact.

Certain locks will be selected regardless of the direction you turn the knob. Some locks (such like those made by Master, for instance) Master brand) like the Master brand, can be opened in any direction and therefore, you should choose the one that is simpler to operate using a torque wrench. Yale padlocks on the however, are only opened when rotated clockwise. Locks which are integrated inside a doorknob or installed in desks, filing cabinets or even drawers typically require a clockwise turn in order to open, whereas single plug Cylinder locks typically open once the top of the keyway (the flat edges of the keys) is swung away from the door frame.

If you're confronted with a brand-new type of lock, turn the plug either way and examine the outcome. A solid stop may occur when the lock is twisted in an incorrect direction. The right direction can result in an unsprung stop in which you can feel pins halting the rotation using the torque.

The Extent of the Plug's Rotation

Once you've decided the direction in which you should change your plug, what degree should you change the plug? A full turn is usually necessary for deadbolt locks however a filing cabinet or desk lock usually needs a 90-degree rotation (a quarter) or less, and so can locks that are built inside the doorknob. The lock is distinct from the doorknob typically needs a half-turn in order for opening it.

Scrubbing Doesn't Set Pins

Scrubbing cannot make the pins set in the lock, despite variations in torque, it's typically the case that one pin was set wrongly that prevents other pins to set. For example, in locks with pins that are set from the front to the back, if one pin fails to set either high or low and the other pins are not able to get set as the plug can't rotate enough to permit the pins to be bonded. In this case it is best to start to focus your attention on the pins in front, using various amounts of torque and pressure until you can feel that the pin is set on the shear lines and feel the slight movement of the plug. A torque wrench that is stiff will help you feel more comfortable about the pin's position.

Springs & Gravity

Some locks have springs in the lower part, while other locks feature them higher up. Locks with springs on the bottom may be simpler to work with, because when you've set the key pins, gravity will hold the pins down. This makes easier to distinguish between unset pins and set ones. This configuration also permits more efficient testing of pins set. Also, gravity is a factor in the event that the springs are on the top. This time, gravity pushes the pins that hold them down when the driver pin is on the shear line. Then, you have to raise the pin in order to verify the pins are set. You can detect the sound of a pin set by using your finger to draw over the pins. They can rattle since the driver pin has stopped pressurizing them.

Elasticity

The driver pin has been set incorrectly through the elasticity

As lock picking requires measures that are in the thousands ofths in an inch, all metals can be elastic, just as springs. This is because just a few pounds of force are needed for directing the metal it will return to its starting point once that force has stopped in its influence. If you'd like more than one pin to be set in a single moment it is possible to use this flexibility to benefit you. If, for instance, you're selecting a lock that has pins are set from front to back you'll notice that the procedure takes a long time, since only each pin is set one in a row if the pressure is only applied upon pulling the lock's pick from the lock. The primary pin is set and other pins may establish the other pins. But, if the plug's holes are just little off from the plug's central point, applying some extra force will cause the plug to twist, which causes the pins on the front to bend enough to allow the back of the plug's cylinder to spin enough that back pins are set. That extra torque could allow for a single stroke of the pick to create multiple pins. This allows your lock to open faster. Insufficient torque or less torque could prevent multiple pins from being set.

Loose Plug

A hole is cut in the hull to hold the plug. It is larger in the front and has a cam at the back which is wider that the opening. There are times when the cam of the lock has not been fitted correctly, which means that the plug can move a little inside the lock. The plug could move as you insert the pick, and the moment you take it off this means driver pins may not be set. These plugs that are loose instead of being fixed to the sides of the holes driver pins usually sit at the rear of the holes. To avoid this you can either secure the plug with your fingers or a torque wrench to ensure that the plug doesn't shift or put pressure on the point of insertion the plug or on the removal of the pick.

Pin Diameter

In some instances pins may possess different diameters that hinder the pins' movements. The key pin could be larger in diameter or it could be the opposite. This is because the pin might stick inside the hull after the pin that sets is not set properly, because the pin may move just enough to secure the smaller key pin while the lock is pressed into the pin that is set. The solution to this problem can be a challenging task for both the experienced and patient lock-picker.

Rounded Pins & Beveled Holes

The sides of the plug holes can be polished in some locks and the edges of key pins can be made rounded to lessen damage that occurs on the lock. It could have one of these characteristics if they have a lot of give. This is because there's a greater gap between the driver pin the plug hole and between the key pin as well as the hull. That means the spring's force is the sole resistance for the pin that travels between these two points and will require lesser forces.

But, a bit more scrub is needed with a beveled plug hole. Because instead of being placed on the side of the plug the driver pins are set on the bevel. That signifies that the plug won't have the ability to turn. In order to move the driver pin away from the bevel, clean the key pin once more.

If the pins appear to be in place inside the lock that has beveled plug holes and however, the lock isn't locked and you're not sure why, try rubbing the pins while decreasing the force, so that drivers will be lifted off the bevels. The pins could be unset if the torque has been reduced. you should increase the pressure on your lock and increase the force and then try it another time.

Mushroom Driver Pins

Lock makers alter the form of the driver pin in order to make it harder to select. It is possible to find the spool, serrated or mushroom designs, that are falsely put them in the pins at a low level. While you won't be able to vibrate pick these pins however, you'll be able to clean the pins and pick each one at a time. Knowing the pins that have been modified is crucial to picking these locks and you must test to see if your locks have modified drivers. The normal driver has the springy giving, whereas an atypical driver doesn't.

It is known that driver's pins can have a different design if you rotate the plug slightly but no pins can be squeezed upwards. The plug will not move, because the driver's lip remains on the line of shear. Apply a small amount of force, press up on the pins; those equipped with drivers for mushroom will secure the plug's location. When you push the pin that you want to use it's flat top presses against the driver's curving bottom. This straightens the driver, and then unwinds the plug. When you know which pin columns trigger the unwinding process, you will be able to identify which ones have drivers for mushroom and move these pins toward that shear line. In the event that, during this process the other pins break, it is possible to repick them less difficult than those with mushroom drivers.

If you've modified your drivers that have been modified, it is recommended to use high pressure on the pick and moderate tension. The pins deeper into the hull, rather than pushing them sufficiently. Another way of approaching altered drivers would be to push the pins to the top using your car's flat surface, and apply more tension to secure them the correct position. After that, gradually decrease the amount of torque in order to lessen the binding friction, and then make the pins vibrate by scratching. Key pins are gradually lowered towards the shear line due to the force of springs and vibrating.

Master Keys

A second pin, also known as an additional pin, also known as a "spacer," is required in certain locks to allow the master key. The change key can open only one lock, whereas master keys open multiple locks. Spacers are included to ensure that both a switch key and master key could be permitted to open the lock. When a spacer is used in the pin column, there are two gaps, which can coincide along the line of shear. The majority of times the master key will draw the lower part of the spacer towards the shear line. On the other hand, the key for change draws its top toward that line. This way the change key can't be sanded down in order to transform it into a bogus master key. Plugs rotate freely regardless of no matter which master or change key is utilized.

In the majority of cases it is possible to pick these locks with less difficulty, because spaces increase the possibilities for setting a pin, and also increases the chances that someone will place all pins at roughly the same level for the lock to be opened. Most of the time, only a few pins have spacers. You can find through a sense of hearing or feeling the pin for two times when you pull the pin back. The most often, the driver pin is smaller than that of the spacer. You can tell due to the increase in friction as the spacer is crossing the shear line. It also enables drivers pins to snag it easier. It is possible to feel a hard click felt when you press the spacer beyond the shear line and into the hull.

In some cases, the key and driver pins are larger in dimensions than the spacer this is evident through the feel because the spacer doesn't connect when it comes across the line of shear. If this is the case, the spacer could get stuck on the shear line when heavy tension is applied, and the holes in the plug are beveled. Spacers can even slide in the keyway when the plug turns to the halfway point. Check out Section 9.11 for solutions to this issue.

Spacer or Driver is in the Keyway

If you turn the plug to halfway the driver pin or spacer could get into the keyway. It is possible to prevent this but by placing your pick's flat end at the lower part of the keyway prior to rotating the plug 180 degrees. Reduce the shear force exerting pressure on the driver or spacer by using the torque wrench using your pick's flat end to push the spacer against the keyway's hull. If the driver or spacer remains inside the keyway area, you can scrub the driver with your pick's pointy side. There may be a need to pull out the spacer by hooking it with a metal clip (or paperclip) in the event that it is completely buried in the keyway.

Vibration Picking

If you create an opening between key and driver pins, it is possible to make use of vibrations to move every pin's tip similar to how the queue ball pushes another ball in a pool. If you hit with a square, the ball is being driven with the same speed like the queue ball travelling, and the queue ball ceases to move on its own. When you vibrate the pins, every key pin is knocked down into the driver pins and then spring them to the top of the hull. Applying a small amount of torque in the same manner the driver pins will be aligned over the shear line and the plug will rotate.

Chapter 8: Tools

If you are advancing to the level of master locks, you must upgrade the tools you use. Below is a comprehensive list of the various tools for picking locks as well as what they could help you.

Torque wrenches

The handpiece that comes with a torque wrench could range between 2 and 4 inches. The head typically is between 1/2 and 3/4 of an inch. The larger the handle, the greater precision you'll be able to manage the torque. However should it be too long, your wrench could hit the door frame. The handle is quite thin, yet it needs to extend beyond protrusions (a lock collar that is grip-proof, as an instance) for it to be inserted into the socket. The width at which the wrench's head can accommodate into the lock will depend on the type of lock. Certain locks, such as file cabinet and desk lock, need an extremely narrow head. A 90-degree angle is the only way to separate the handle from the head. Some feature a twisting that is 90 degrees. This creates the handle as a spring and makes making it easier to control the torque. By twisting the handle but not have as much of a feeling in the rotation of the plug.

Make the torque wrench of your choice using eight-penny nails with a diameter in the range of .1 inch. By using a propane torch, or gas stove heat the wrench's tip until it's glowing red. Remove it out of the flame slowly then allow it to become cool and soft. After that, you can grind it to form a small screwdriver-shaped blade by bending it to 80 degrees. Don't bend it at an exact angle as the wrench's head must extend to a minimum of a half-inch to the end of the plug. Moreover, plates can recess the lock's face, limiting the reach. Then, use your wrench until it is orange, and then immerse into ice water to temper or harden your tool. This torque wrench is extremely durable and will last for long time to in the future.

Pick Shapes

There are numerous types and sizes of picks you can choose from but the tang and the handle are one and the same. The tang needs to be minimal in order to not impact the pins. However, it should be not so thin that it'll feel similar to a spring which will make it difficult to get a precise feel of the pick's impact on the pins. The handle must be comfortable and easy for use.

The point of the pick's form will decide how much you feel pins as well as the speed at which it crosses pins. The design of the tip will lead you to the tip suitable for your needs and to open the lock. As an example locks with pins each side of the keys most effective when opened with the full diamond or full round tip. On the other hand, a disk tumbler lock should be open using a half-round. If you must pick pins at once or rub them over using a rake, the tip that you use is ideal. When you do this just apply pressure only when you remove the pin. It is useful if you don't want to leave marks of your pick, as it is aligned with the pin, and thus does not scratch pins and disperse metal dust, particularly when you pick one-by-1. The rake tip can be straight or dented the rake tip.

If you're not worried about leaving footprints, it's best to clean this method, which is ideal to open locks for your home with five pins. The snake tip may also be used to pick; it will set multiple pins in one go as when you lower or raise the tips the point acts like a key piece by using powerful force.

Half diamond tips for picks, such as those, can be either sharp or narrow. They offer a greater feel on the pins. Meanwhile, smaller angles make it easier to insert and removal. They allow users to put pressure on the lock in any the other way. If there is a small variation between the key pins of a lock the narrow angled tips is able to pick locks easily but if the lock has a lot of variations such as a dip that is deep between two dips that are shallow - the middle pin might not be easily pushed downwards using a narrow-angled tip and a sharp-angled tip is the best option. An angled-up tip comes with its downsides as well; it could be harder to control inside the lock.

If you're looking for an unorthodox pick, consider with a bicycle wheel by just bending it into the desired size as well as filing one side to flat. The horizontal part of the tool is supposed to be pliable, but it's vertical is strong. The pick can be bent into an inch triangle to make the shape of a handle.

Chapter 9: Mechanisms

To be able to choose a lock, it's helpful to comprehend how it works. The most common types of locks that will be covered below are Warded, pin tumbler, Wife/Disc Tumbler Lever, and Combination.

Before I discuss how various locks operate I'll begin by describing the fundamental components of a lock. I will also give additional information that can help users comprehend the information provided.

The most simple lock to grasp and pick can be the one with a warded lock and that's where I'll begin.

Warded Locks

The lock that is warded has an easy style.

Below is a diagram of the basic warded lock, with the correct key in its place. The diagram shows this diagram that the lock contains a series of cuts within it that allow keys to go through the metal pieces that protrude. The metal pieces are the main wards for the lock. They will change in size and location.

The lock is equipped with at least one or two "wards," which stop an wrong key from throwing the bolt. Wards extend within the lock, preventing an untrue key from turning, and thus inoperating the bolt.

The warded lock is located in various varieties. This diagram will show what the mechanism of the warded lock may be located in various types. This diagram shows how a warded padlock functions. They're typically the least priced padlocks.

Pin Tumbler Locks

The interior of the inside of a pin tumbler lock may be observed from the illustration below.

Pin tumbler locks is made up of two sets of pins on the bottom generally constructed of brass, as well as top drivers that are made from steel. For the vast majority of locks, you will find five drivers and pins.

Once the right key has been put into the lock, that point at which pins at the top and bottom are separated will be brought back to the same location. This is referred to as the shear point, also known as the shearing line. If this point is reached, the cylinder is allowed to rotate, and then the lock will be opened.

This lock has the wrong key put in. The key isn't raising some pins up at the proper height, as well as elevated some pins to a higher level. This means that the cylinder is not able to rotate.

A lot of high-security locks employ the mushroom pin or spool pin for making picking these locks tougher. It is evident in the image below.

Pins with the shape illustrated above make it more difficult to pick pin tumbler locks because they make it appear that when you pick the lock it appears that the pin has been inserted. However, the pin has not stopped the cylinder from turning, however the recess for the pins with high security allows the cylinder's cylinder to spin creating the illusion that the certain pins have been elevated to the proper size.

Wafer Locks

The locks are located on desks, filing cabinets, a few coin-operated devices, as well as on the doors to cars. Though it is similar as pin tumbler locks, their mechanism inside is distinct.

This diagram shows the insides of an ordinary wafer lock.

The disc tumblers, also known as wafers are essentially metal discs with a one rectangular hole at the middle. In a lock made of wafers, typically, there are five discs, based on the level of security in the lock. If a key is put into a lock made of wafers, it will go through this opening.

The opposite side of the disc there is an elongated spring. The discs lock when the spring forces the disc downwards through top of the cylinder into the casing that surrounds the lock. The key's purpose is to elevate the discs out of their casing until the wafer will be at the center of the cylindrical. If a key were to elevate a wafer far, the cylinder could become inoperable as the disc will protrude out of the upper part of the cylinder.

The locks for wafers can come in either one or double-sided. Double-sided locks offer more protection than a one sided lock. They can also be located on cars. The discs on double-sided locks will extend through the sides and the top of the cylindrical. This is due to the fact that the discs will be placed in the first wafer, having the spring force it down. A second spring in the wafer will push it up. Third one will be forcibly down. The alternating pattern continues based on the wafer count within the lock.

The lock with a double-sided blade is distinguished from the typical single-sided lock because keys will feature nodes on both edges of the blade.

Chapter 10: Lever Lock

The type of lock is comprised typically of four or five levers. The typical lever is found below.

Each lever is elevated up to different levels through the use of a key, which permits the notch on the lever to be aligned with the posts of the bolt. The key is still turning which allows the bolt to move through the notch, where it eventually rests at the other gate after having turned 360 degrees.

This kind of lock is offered in two varieties. They each operate with keys of a different kind. The majority of door locks in the UK are for example, using the bit type key. While lever locks on suitcases, lockers and desks utilize keys of a flat design but the basic principle for each is identical.

Combination Locks

Combination locks are available in various designs and can be used on padlocks as well as brief cases. It could be the dial style that is similar to the security lock found in a safe or could be made up of smaller disks, each one with a number that are to be positioned in a specific sequence to enable the lock unlock. It could also include a press button type as is found in a variety of padlocks.

The underlying principle for the three types is the similar, i.e. connecting gates from different elements of the lock order to allow the bolt to be moved, the layout of each style is different and therefore will be addressed independently.

Dial Combination

The type of combination lock is comprised of a dial located that is located on the front of the lock. It typically, it will have a type of mark or an arrow to one side. The arrow will indicate the different numbers at the top of the dial. To open the lock, the dial have to be rotated multiple times, clockwise and counterclockwise to align the arrow with an alternate number every moment until the lock is able to open.

Within this lock, there are several discs typically around 2 based on the numbers used in the combo. Every disc is the appearance of a gate or notch that is cut out of the disc. The reason for this gate is that, when the dial has turned in the right order, the bolt that holds the shackle to its place is allowed to slide through the opening created through these gates, thereby freeing the shackle, allowing the padlock to be opened. Below is a diagram of inside the typical combination padlock of this kind without the front from the lock, where the disc and bolt are visible set in the right place.

The surface of the disc that runs to its back is a protrusion that will be caught by an identical protrusion to the bottom of the second disc. The second disk will feature a tiny protrusion in its surface that will be caught by an elongated protrusion behind the dial. As the dial rotates, the underside of its protrusion is able to contact the protrusion of the first disk and it will rotate. The process will then turn the second disk when the protrusion that is on the bottom of the disk in contact with that on the surface of the second, and makes the two disks move together. The dial will be rotated in this direction, the dial will be

The disks should be rotated just the correct amounts to line the gates of every disk by securing the bolt that allows it to come away from the shackle, unlocking the lock.

There are two primary varieties of dial padlocks which will affect the manner in the way it is chosen, which will be explained in the future. What makes them differ lies in how the bolt which locks the shackle is made. Some older lock types were snapped they were opened once the dial been rotated, despite the fact that the gate's position weren't in the same position. The reason for this was because the bolt being fitted with the spring-loaded part of it as shown illustrated in the above diagram. It meant that after the lock was opened and the dial turned, rearranging the gate's position and thus moving the bolt in to the shackle's direction, the shackle would be moved down, thereby moving the spring-loaded component inwards, which then expand outwards to the shackle's notch and lock the padlock.

However, the new design is not equipped with this spring-loaded part of the bolt. Instead, it is entirely solid. Thus, when the padlock opens when the dial turns, the bolt is forced through the gate, and the padlock won't be in no position to force it inside the lock.

Disk combination

This particular type of combination can be seen on many bicycle chains as well as short cases, as well as on various types of padlocks. look below for.

This diagram depicts this kind of lock at its simplistic form. It is a basic bicycle lock. The concept behind locks is the same for any lock of this type in spite of a few distinctions in their construction in the present and future.

The primary difference in their design is the lock's combination is able to be altered. This article will begin by discussing the basics of locks with an ordinary factory set combination that is much less complicated in construction. I will be able to explain later the more intricate design that permits the keeper or the owner of the lock modify the combination as is possible in the case of short cases, for instance.

Each type of lock will be made up of several discs, which are numbered along their outside edges. With the lock that is not able to have the combination altered, there will be a notched located inside, just behind an digit from the disc. When these notch align that a portion of the lock is moved, thus unlocking the lock. For the chains on bicycles, as an example, one side of the chain is the lock and the other part is an elongated plug that has a couple of pegs that are small on the edge. They will be sufficient to pass across the notches on the discs.

Once the lock has been locked, the plug is fixed, which places those pegs in front of each disc, and not be able to move due to the solid parts of each disc. But, if the discs are in proper order, the notches will be placed in the same place as the pegs which will allow the plug to fall out.

The exact same concept of the bicycle lock can be found in locks that could use a shackle in place of an outlet like various varieties of bicycle locks, and padlocks. This diagram shows an alternative sort of bicycle chain which is equipped with the shackle as well as padlocks.

The main difference between the bike lock that was described earlier as well as the locks that have the shackles lies in that there is an element of the shackle with pegs which allow the shackle to be locked instead of plug.

Combination disc locks that are able to be altered are built differently in it's not the disc that is notch-free it is a distinct component in the process.

This diagram shows how internal functions work in an uncomplicated case lock. the various parts labeled.

The separate components of a lock tend to be smaller discs that instead of having a cut from its inside, will have a notch removed on the outside (see earlier).

The case is locked by the grid that is attached to the bolt. It is connected to the button that pushes outwards to unlock the lock. This grid is positioned around the metal, and as well as the plastic discs, and secures the case because the discs made of plastic will extend across the grid.

If the correct sequence has been entered, the metallic numbering discs in turn will spin the discs made of plastic to where an element has been taken away. So the plastic discs not protrude from this grid. They will also allow the bolt and grid to rotate, opening the box.

For the purpose of changing the key combination for a short case lock, a tiny switch is placed to the inside of the case. The result is the rod being moved along with the plastic discs. Thus, if the numbered discs are rotated now, they are not affecting the discs made of plastic, which remain the same way which allows a different combination to be selected. If the switch located within the case is moved again the rod is able to slide backwards and the discs will slide into the numbered discs this time around an angle that will allow the grid to expand which is where the numbers for the combination that is being chosen will be.

Push Button Combination

The type of combination lock is illustrated in the image below.

If the right numbers of buttons are pressed, the button on the bottom of the lock will be in a position to rotate and the shackle snaps to open. The lock is made up of a grid that is moved when it opens the lock. Notches cut out of the buttons allow the grid to move and, consequently, allow it will be able to open. This is also where the notches are situated on every button, which determines the lock's combination.

The numbers that do not constitute a part of the lock will feature notches that are already lined up with the grid. However the notches on the buttons that form the key combination will only align once they're pressed, thus permitting the lock to be opened.

Tools

For you to successfully open the lock, it is essential to use the correct tools to do the task.

This article will show you which tools you need to use for the lock you're trying to break.

Chapter 11: Warded

A majority of the locked that are warded come as padlocks. The equipment required for locks can be constructed or bought for a small costs. These being skeleton keys. This kind of lock is the only one that can be used with skeleton keys. It is important to be understood what a skeleton key really is to debunk any misconceptions regarding these keys.

The skeleton key is an uncut key that is made up of the metal needed to open the lock. When you look at the lock that is warded, looking at the mechanisms section, it's observed that a portion of the lock is not moving, i.e. the ward itself. That's where a key, with just enough metal for the locking component, enters. Below is a diagram of the operation and function of the Skeleton Key.

It is evident that an area of the key has been shaved away, preventing the key from being blocked from the ward and leaving the end of the key to be able to contact the mechanism that locks and then open the lock.

The skeleton keys can be obtained for very little money, but they can be created with minimal effort. Keys that skeletonize for the particular model of locked that is warded to open others locks of the same series is made quickly by taking a portion of the key that could be blocked by the lock's ward. This diagram shows the way a key for the lock could be created to unlock other locks in similar series, and also secured locks from other brands.

Pin Tumbler & Wafer

The tools needed to open the two kinds of locks are the same which is why they are examined in conjunction.

Contrary what is believed There aren't any keys that unlock this lock, as depicted in the films. It it is more a matter of skills and training.

Hook Picks

They are intended for use of "pure picking" as described in the sections on techniques.

What is required here is to comprehend what they're about and be aware that they are available in various sizes.

Rakes

Rakes are available in a range of forms and sizes. Below is a diagram of some of the more popular.

Turning Tools/Tension Wrench

Bypass Pick

The tool is easily constructed by grinding a saw blade until it reaches a point like the one shown below.

Lever

Lifter Picks

The amount of this can be decided by the lever lock that is to be pulled.

Turning Tool/Tension Wrench

The tool, though it has the same name employed for wafer and pin locks, is quite different in its construction. In terms of form as well as the quality of the steel used. The reasons behind this is to be explained in the section on methods.

Combination Brief Case

Combination Probe

The type of probe does not need the same strength as the same bypass pick that is used to pin tumbler locks, but should be very thin.

This probe has only the reason of opening briefcase combination locks.

The probe I designed to use in this experiment was constructed out of a gauge for a feeling. Particularly,

a number 12

Constructing Picks

While they are not expensive to purchase, they can be a challenge to obtain these items and find outlets that can sell them.

It is not an issue as the right selections are able to be made on your own with effort and perseverance.

To make the perfect pick, it's an absolute requirement to possess a grinder as grinding tools cannot shape the necessary metal to produce an enduring and durable pick.

That brings us to the most important question, i.e., what metal is best to use and how can it be found? In order for the metal you choose to be useful, it should meet two primary specifications. It has to be durable and slim, (to get past any fancy keyhole that is between the user and device).

This kind of metal is easily located in hacksaw blades. They are able to be marked with the form of picks through making use of a permanent pen and then cut with precision to get the form needed. The metal can be extremely beneficial and is able to make hooks, rakes and picks. bypass picks, as well as lever lock lifter pick.

Sets of gauges for feelers, are available at hardware or automotive shops, can also supply metal that can be utilized. Though some can only be used for shims, they are also able to be used as probes or picks (especially combinations probes) according to their thickness and strength.

The material used to make the turning tool, for both wafer/pin tumbler and for levers is different. To turn a tool for opening a pin tumbler/wafer stop any springy metal that can be bent into the above-depicted shape, i.e, the straight straightforward simple turning tool of type A that is not changing its form, will be adequate.

Lever lock tool should be made of an extremely robust and durable steel. It must be constructed in a way that when it's in its desired design, it won't bend. it can generate a powerful turn force.

Warded

The process of opening padlocks is discussed in the tool section. The manner in that these locks can be unlocked is via a the skeleton key. What's left to do is test each key you have that you have, regardless of whether purchased or made by you, after inserting the key into the lock to as close as is possible. If you are unsuccessful in unlocking the lock, take the key from the lock and twist the key back.

In accordance with the amount of keys you have in your collection, it is possible to open a wide range of locks at a minimum effort by testing every key in this manner.

Chapter 12: Pin Tumbler As Well As Wafer
Pure Picking

This method of picking demands the use of more skills, patience and experience than the other method, however when you master it, it is a highly effective method for completing.

This way of opening may be utilized on the pin tumbler as well as the wafer lock, and requires the use of hook picks.

The first thing to do is put the hookpick in the lock to ensure that it is inserted completely into the lock.

The tool to turn is put into the keyway, and the tool is gently turned. It is only a slight pressurization is required, otherwise the pins could bind, i.e. the lock would become jammed. the lock.

When the turning tool is pressed, rotating tool, a slight pushing motion is applied to the tool to gradually lift the pin that is at the bottom. The goal, it must be mentioned is to lift all pins on the top into the top chambers in the lock. So, the lower pins must be allowed to sink back to the lower casing after the pick has been moved onto the following pin. The lower pin shouldn't be lifted above the shear lines. While lifting the driver pin and lower pins, at the point when the top of the lowest pin touches the shear line, a quick click will be heard and the pin should lose any spring.

After this has been felt, slide the pin down and towards the rear of the lock, so that contact with the pin is made. A similar prying motion and sensitivity is required. Keep going until all pins have reached the shear line, at which point the lock finally gives.

In the course of this process, the only gentle movement has been made.

Raking

If you can master this technique well, will be probably the most efficient method to unlock the pin tumbler or wafer lock.

The idea behind this method is that it causes the pins to move, making them bounce around on the line of shear. The result is that certain top drivers to come off the plug but others will remain to the plug. This method makes the pins raised in an erratic manner which means that they are not a perfect match. With different shapes of rakes, the lift pattern is different and the chance of effectiveness rate increases.

Raking can also be effective on locks for wafers. Ragging will cause the wafers to move up and down, and find the right places that will enable the cylinder turn.

The rake must be positioned on the rear to the back of the lock. The turning tool should be in the keyway however the pressure does not get put on it. This is the only time that the tool is released from the lock that tension, which is a light tension is put on it.

Each rake needs to be used for at least 15 times before you find a new one that works.

Bypassing

The method is used with padlocks, as well as filing cabinets that are secured by a pin that protrudes from an upper portion or the bottom.

The bypass pick that is shown in the Tools section can be utilized. This method is easy and reliable since it doesn't require the skills required by the two above methods. All that is required is knowledge of the purpose for which the bypass pick does, that the diagram below will be able to demonstrate.

Shimming is a method to unlock padlocks secured by a pin tumbler. It also eliminates the need pick the lock. This is done by simply attacking the area of the lock that locks the shackle.

The following diagram illustrates how the shim works to unlock the Shackle.

Lever

The lock type is used extensively across the UK for door locks as well as padlocks.

In order to open this kind lock, a pick for lifting and turning tool, as detailed in the section on tools are necessary.

The tool is used to apply a continuous pressure to the bolt that locks during the raising of levers.

The lifting tool lifts every lever, and when it has been elevated to the right height will remain in position due to the strength of the bolt that is caused by the pressure created by the force of the tool for turning. So, a sturdy turning tool is required because the springs on the levers is not easily removed, thereby restoring each lever to its normal location once the pick was taken away.

The pick that lifts the lever is able to be positioned at the right of the lock, lifting every lever at a time but I like to raise the lever that is the most difficult to raise in the beginning, which allows the bolt to put more force on the other levers when they are elevated.

When a lever has been elevated to the proper height, there ought to be a little tension in the bolt since it will have just one lever to stop the lever from sliding. Lever that is raised should also be simpler to move because the edge of the bolt won't be in contact with it due to it being within its gate.

You can move on to the next lever, whether it is that next lever on the line, or the one you find the hardest to get around. At this point, less pressure must be applied to the tension wrench, but make sure that you don't let the first lever fall into the original location. The second lever(s) are able to be pulled using the same method until the bolt moves through the entire length and the lock is opened.

Padlocks

Dial

A lot of padlocks use an arrangement in the shape of a dial like in the image below.

The manner in which the lock functions has been covered in the article of mechanisms, so once you have a better understanding of how they can be opened will be clarified.

It should be noted that the purpose of you do by turning the dial in a proper sequence is to put all the gates in the same location which allows for the bolt to slip in it, which allows the shackle to raise it up.

For opening this lock, the first step you need to do is place an upward pressure to the shackle. The method is to hold the lock with your less strong hand, and then placing your finger beneath the shackle before pushing it to move upwards. This will trigger the bolt that is locking the shackle to move up. This will cause the part that is locked to be able to move into the space created by gates to be rubbing against the wheels, and thus result in friction. It is expected that in theoretical terms, when this locking element is at the gate, the dial will thump, and eventually become stiffer. As a result of other wheels pressing against this locking element and thus limiting the movement of the bolt of locking, the feel of this thump, and the absence of friction is slightly diminished.

That's why it's essential to pay attention and being able to feel the moment the gates have been reached. Additionally, it may be helpful placing the lock in front of your ear as you turn the dial to be able to hear clearly the moment where the thump takes place.

Once the initial number has been achieved, the dial has to be rotated in the reverse direction for 1 full turn, and the same procedure is followed to detect the number two.

The number 3 can be located easily the number is found, when you change the direction of the dial for a 2nd time. After that, the shackle is expected to be able to open. The number could make the dial, upon it is first turning, to stop and make a click that is quite loud, and cannot be confused with the number that was first rung.

Dial: With Push Closed Clasp

While these locks may be opened the same manner as described in the previous paragraph, due to their capacity to the door shut, it makes them accessible to a technique that eliminates the requirement to use the sensitivity technique previously mentioned. This allows them to be opened faster and easier.

The way these could be opened is shifting. Shimming is the process of inserting a shim down the inside of the shackle and pull the bolt to backwards.

In the case of a non-snap-closed lock, after the dial is turned in the proper sequence, and the shackle remains opened, if the dial was to be rotated with the shackle in an non-locked position, the lock will be in a position not to be locked since the bolt will not be able to retract.

But, here's the area where the snap-closed padlock is different, because when the dial has been moved with the shackle removed of the lock, it is able to be locked again because the bolt can spring to its original position when the shackle has been placed in the lock.

Below is a diagram that illustrates the differences between the locking bolts used for snap-closed locks and snap-closed locks.

A lot of combination dial locks come with circular bodies and provide ease of access to the bolt that is spring loaded.

Another thing to be taken into consideration when it comes to dial lock. The reason is that after someone has secured the shackle, they often do not move the dial to enough so that it alters the location of all the locks' wheels. Thus, locks like this one can usually be opened quickly simply turning the dial counterclockwise slow. The reason for this is that most users are left-handed and thus will be able to rotate the dial when they lock the lock clockwise. Since they can only turn about half of a revolution, the only wheel that can move will be the top wheel and will not affect the other places that the gate is in. So, when you turn the dial again in the reverse direction, it will replace the gate to the correct position that allows the bolt to move, and the lock to unlock.

Push Button

The padlock of this kind is fairly modern. The illustration can be seen in the following image.

It can be opened the following manner.

By applying tension to the knob at the bottom of the lock, push the button to the left side to the downwards. The buttons will be marked 1-5.

All numbers include gates that let a grid within to move. This slide action happens when the button located at the base is released which moves the bolt from the shackle. However, the buttons stop this movement, thus keeping the shackle.

A correct combination allows the grid within to move since the gates/notches that are at the top of each button will appear in the top of the buttons than those buttons which don't belong to the combo. Thus, by using the correct combination, what will happen is that the gates are aligned, which allows that the grid's position to change as well as the bolt to break away from the shackle.

In the course of picking this kind of lock, once the buttons have been moved down, if the appropriate tension to the button's base, you will notice that a few of the numbered buttons are not lower as low as they can be. The reason is that they have gates that are lower, and are not an integral part of the system.

So, if you applied tension on the slide when they were in the up position, it resulted in the grid being forced to go into gates a little, thus limiting the movement of these gates downwards. The next step is increase the numbers that didn't fall completely into the lock because most of the sequence was found. You have to remove those numbers that aren't part of the sequence.

The next thing to do is press down without tension on the next column of numbers i.e. 6-0. Then, by applying pressure to the sliding button, all you have to do is slowly push upwards the buttons in a sequence. Since the buttons that are included in the combination have gates that are in align with the grid, and the consequence of applying pressure on the slide tends to stop their movements upwards. But the numbers that do not form part of the combo however they are able to move up. The only thing left to be done is to make sure that all buttons that make up the combination are depressed completely and that all numbers that do not form part of the combo are removed from the lock. The lock must now give.

Disk

The padlock type can be observed in the picture below.

Another key for opening this lock like many combination locks is applying pressure.

The force should be applied to the shackle, which will result in making one of the disks get rigid and difficult to turn. This disk is the first to be dealt with. It is all that is needed is to rotate the disk, while keeping the tension on the shackle until the tension has been released. That is the moment where the section of the shackle that was blocked from moving across the disk will now be able to move through since the gate will be in the same position.

The correct information on the first disk you have worked on will result in tension which can then be applied to one of the disks. The exact number on the disk is found using the same method that you used previously.

Because these kinds of locks have only three disks the only thing you have to accomplish is turn the last disk to ensure that the lock opens when you are pulling on the Shackle.

Chapter 13: Bicycle Chain

The image will likely appear in one of the two images that are below.

They can be opened similar fashion to the disk padlock described earlier.

Some important things must be taken note of. Tension is required to allow to determine which gates are in the right place. Because the gates represent points within the disks, where no metal is present in the disks, the corresponding peg on the shackle is no longer going to cause tension, and becomes loose.

But, because of the additional disks that are taking on the tension when the first one has been identified, it could frequently be difficult to perceive. The practice of this can pay off since this distinctness will be easily discernible.

Brief Case

The lock described above can be easily unlocked using the specially-designed tool. This tool was discussed in the section on tools and therefore reference to it is required.

The mechanism of this kind of lock needs to be thoroughly comprehended in order to unlock it. Thus, one should look back at the mechanics section, where the lock was described. Like all locks it is the best method to know the mechanism of a lock is to take it apart your self, which is not enough to be discussed.

When the internal functioning of the lock is scrutinized, you will see that at the exact point you can find the correct number an nipper is found. That is the notch that the probe or probe is trying to locate. It is also smaller than the other parts of the disk, so it can also be felt. right side. The correct place to put it on. It is located to the right side of the dial that is the furthest from the button, and closest to the havep. The probe is to be put on the sides of the disk until it comes into contact by the ring made of plastic that the disk sits upon. The plastic ring turns with the metal ring because of projections of it that form the form of a star. On this particular the ring, there is a smooth area that is right next to the numbers of the combination. This is exactly what the probe tool seeks to locate by insertion into the inside of each disk.

Chapter 14: Mechanisms

To be able to choose a lock, it's helpful to comprehend the mechanism of the lock. The principal types of lock we will discuss below are Warded, pin tumbler and Wafer/Disc Tumbler Lever, Combination and.

However, before I go into the details of how various types of locks function, I'll begin by describing the fundamental components of a lock. Then, I'll offer additional details that will help the reader comprehend the information provided.

The easiest lock to grasp and pick can be the one with a warded lock this is the place I'll begin.

Warded Locks

The lock that is warded has an extremely straightforward layout.

Below is a diagram of an easy warded lock that has the correct key in its place. The diagram shows this diagram that the lock is made with a variety of cut within it that allow keys to go through the protruding metal pieces. The metal pieces are the main wards for the lock. They will change in size and location.

The lock is equipped with several 'wards to stop the wrong key from dislodging the bolt. Wards extend in the lock to prevent an untrue key from turning it and, consequently inoperating the bolt.

The warded lock is located in various varieties. The following diagram demonstrates the different ways that warded locks can be seen in a variety of varieties. The following diagram demonstrates the way a warded padlock operates. They are typically the cheapest priced padlocks.

Pin Tumbler Locks

The insides of the pin tumbler lock could be observed from the illustration below.

A pin tumbler lock comprises of of bottom pins that are typically constructed from brass and top drivers that are made from steel. For the vast majority of locks, you will find five pins as well as drivers.

If the key that is correct has been in the lock, that point where top and bottom pins are separated will be brought back to the same place. The position is known as the shear point, also known as the shearing line. Once this line is attained, the cylinder is allowed to rotate and then the lock will be opened.

The lock below was inserted with an incorrect key installed. It is evident that the key isn't raising certain pins to the correct level as well as raised some pins to a higher height. Thus, the cylinder becomes not able to rotate.

A lot of high-security locks employ the mushroom pin or spool pin for making picking these locks more difficult. It is evident in the image below.

The pins in the forms illustrated above make it more difficult to pick lock pins because they make it appear upon picking the lock it appears that the pin has been removed. The pin has not stopped the cylinder from rotating but the recess for high security pins permits the cylinder to rotate slightly and give the impression that a certain pins have been elevated to the proper level.

Many clear-practice locks as well as cutaway locks can also be found for purchase. They allow you to see the pins in a direct way that you choose.

Wafer Locks

The locks are commonly found on desks, file cabinets, a few coin-operated machines, and even on the automobile doors. While it looks similar as pin tumbler locks, their inner mechanism is quite distinct.

Below is a diagram of the insides of one of these locks.

The disc tumblers, also known as wafers are just metal discs that have a an opening that is rectangular in the middle. In a lock made of wafers, typically, there are five discs, based on the level of security in the lock. When a key is placed into a lock made of wafers, it will go through this opening.

On the other edge of every disc there is the spring. The discs lock when the spring forces this disc downwards into the bottom of the cylindrical cylinder, and then into the outer enclosure of the lock.

The key's purpose is to elevate every disc in the casing to ensure that the wafer will be at the center of the cylindrical. If the purpose of the key is to elevate a wafer far, the cylinder could become inoperable as the disc will protrude out of the cylinder's top rather than.

The locks for wafers can come in any of two kinds, one or double-sided. Double-sided locks offer more protection than a one double sided lock. They can also be located on cars. The discs in the double-sided lock extend through the sides and the top of the cylindrical. The reason for this is that the discs are arranged on the top of the first one and the spring pushing it to move downwards. A second spring in the wafer will push it up. The third one is forcibly to the downwards. The pattern of alternating is dependent on the wafers that are in the lock.

The lock with a double-sided blade is distinguished from a more typical single-sided lock because the keys have two notches along the edges of the blade.

Chapter 15: Lever Lock

This kind of lock is comprised typically of four or five levers. The typical lever is located below.

Every lever is raised up to different levels via the key that allows the notch of the lever to line up with the posts of the bolt. The key is still turning and thus rotates the bolt that locks it into the notch until it eventually rests inside the second gate after having turned 360 degrees.

The lock is available in two types. Both are operated using keys of a different kind. The majority of door locks in the UK are for example, using the bit type key. While lever locks in suitcases, lockers and desks utilize a flat key but the underlying principle of every type of lock is the identical.

Combination Locks

Combination locks come in various designs and can be seen on padlocks and short cases. It could be an engraved dial like the security lock found in a safe or it could comprise smaller disks, each one with a number that are to be placed in the correct sequence to enable the lock unlock. A combination lock could comprise a type that has a push button, as seen in various padlocks.

While the basic principle of the three types is the similar, i.e. the lining of gates on different components of the lock in order to allow the bolt to be moved, the layout of each style is different which is why they will be reviewed independently.

Dial Combination

The type of combination lock has an incredibly small dial that is placed in the center of the lock. It typically, it will have some kind marking or an arrow to the side.

The arrow will indicate the different numbers that are located on the edges of the dial. To unlock the lock, the dial require turning multiple times, clockwise and counterclockwise by aligning the arrow to an alternate number every moment until the lock opens.

In this lock is several discs typically around 2 depending on the numbers that are in the combination. Each disc has small gate or notch made from the disc. The reason for this gate is to ensure that once the dial is rotated according to the proper sequence and the bolt that will keep the shackle locked to the shackle will be able to pass through the opening that these gates create, opening the shackle, allowing the padlock's door to swing open. Below is a diagram of inside the typical combination padlock of this kind without the front with a disc, and a bolt are seen on the inside.

Surrounding the disk toward the rear of the lock, there will be the protrusion of a tiny size that is able to catch a similar one to the bottom of the second disc. Also, the second disk will feature a tiny protrusion across its face that will be caught by a protrusion that is located at the rear of the dial. If the dial is turned the protrusion that is on its bottom will meet that protrusion from the previous disk, causing it to rotate. The process will then move the second disk because the protrusion that is on the bottom of the disk in contact with the protrusion on the surface of the second, and makes the two disks move together. As the dial is moved in the

In the correct order, the disks will be rotated just the correct quantity to align the gates on each disk, thereby that allows it to come from the shackle before open the lock.

There are two primary kinds of dial padlocks that will affect the manner in how it's selected, and are discussed in the following paragraphs. What makes them differ lies in how the bolt that locks the shackle was constructed. A lot of older locks of this kind could be easily snapped opened after the dial been rotated, even though gates was no longer in the same position. The reason for this was because the bolt being fitted with an element that was spring loaded to it, like in the picture above. It meant that after the lock was open and the dial was rotated, changing the positions of the gates which in turn moved the bolt back into to the shackle's direction, the shackle would be pulled upwards, which would then move this spring loaded component inwards, which then extend outwards and into the shackle's notch which would then lock the padlock.

The latest design however doesn't use the spring-loaded part of the bolt, which instead is totally solid. So, once the padlock opens when the dial turns, the bolt is forced away from the gate and the padlock is in no position to force it inside the lock.

Disk combination

This particular type of combination can be present on numerous bicycle chains as well as brief cases as well as various types of padlocks. check below.

The illustration shows this sort of lock, in the basic form: a bicycle lock. The idea behind locks is the same for every lock in this style in spite of a few variations in their design in the present and future.

One of the main differences between them in design is the lock's combination is able to be altered. We will start by examining the fundamental design of a lock that has an ordinary factory set combination which is much less complicated to build and be able to explain later the more intricate model that allows owners of locks to modify the combination such as with brief cases, such as.

The two types of locks be made up of several discs, which are numbered at their edges. With the lock that is not able to have the combination altered, there is a cut located inside, just behind an digit on the disc. When these notch are aligned that the part of the lock is moved, thereby unlocking the lock. For the chains on bicycles, as an example, one side of the chain will be the lock while the other is connected to a plug, which has a set of pegs that are small on the edge. They will be big enough to fit between the notches on discs.

Once the lock has been locked, the plug is set, putting the pegs on each disc, and remain in place because of the solid portion that the discs. But, if the discs are placed in proper order, they will have the notch placed exactly where the pegs are, which will allow the plug to fall out.

The exact same concept of a bicycle lock is also applicable to locks that may use a shackle in place of plugs, like different varieties of bicycle locks, and padlocks. This diagram shows another kind of chain for bicycles, one that has an shackle and a padlock.

The main difference between the bicycle lock described above and locks equipped with Shackles is that it is an element of the shackle that has the pegs which allow the shackle lock instead of plug.

Combination disc locks that are able to be altered are built differently the reason being that it's not the disc in itself that is notch-free it is a distinct component in the process.

This diagram shows how the insides work of a case lock, with the various components labeled.

The separate components of a lock tend to be smaller discs, which rather than being fitted with a hole at its innermost part, they will have a gap removed on the outside (see the previous paragraph).

The case is locked by a tiny grid, which is attached to the bolt. It is linked to the button, which can be pushed upwards in order to open the lock. The grid can be fitted around the metal as well as the plastic discs, that lock the case since discs made of plastic will extend across the grid.

Once the right combination has been entered, the discs made of metal will spin the discs of plastic to the point where the part is taken away. Thus, the discs made of plastic will be unable to protrude past this grid. They will also allow the bolt and grid to open the casing.

For the purpose of changing the lock's combination, a simple key lock in the case, a switch is moved to within the interior of the casing. It is a result of the rod being moved along with the plastic discs. Thus, if the numbered discs are rotated now, they are not affecting the discs made of plastic, which remain at the same place which allows a different combination to be picked. Once the switch in the case moves again, the rod is able to slide backwards and the discs will be inserted into the number discs this time around the point that allows the grid to be opened which is where the numbers for the new combo appear.

Push Button Combination

This kind of combination lock is illustrated in the figure below.

If the right numbers of buttons are pressed, the switch at the base of the lock is able to be moved and the shackle snaps shut. This kind of lock consists of a grid, which is moved when it opens the lock. Notches cut out of the buttons permit this grid to move, thus, the lock to open. The key is to know where the notches are placed on each button that decides the locking combination.

The numbers that don't make up the lock will be engraved with notches, which are aligned with the grid. However the notch on the keys that make up the lock will align once they're pressed, thus opening the lock.

Tools

For you to successfully open the lock, it is essential to use the correct equipment.

This section will help you understand the tools required to open the specific lock you're trying to break.

Warded

A majority of the locked that are warded come from padlocks. Tools needed to make lock are constructed or bought for a small costs. These being skeleton keys. The lock described above is the only one that can be used with skeleton keys. In this case, it must be recalled what a key is actually in order to debunk any misconceptions regarding the keys.

The skeleton key is an uncut key that is made up of sufficient metal to unlock the lock. In the case of a warded lock in relation to the mechanism section, it's noticed that the lock is not moving, i.e. the part that actually wards. That's where a key, with just enough metal for the locking portion, is used. This diagram illustrates how to operate the key with a skeleton.

It can be observed that an area of the key has been shaved away, preventing the key from getting stopped from the ward and permitting the other end to be able to contact the mechanism for locking and thus unlock the lock.

Skeletal keys are purchased for a reasonable price, but they are also able to be created with minimal effort. Keys that skeletonize for the particular model of secured lock that opens the others locks of the same series can be created easy by simply removing a part of the key that could be blocked by the lock's ward. This diagram shows the way a key for the lock could be created to unlock other locks in similar series, and also locked warded by other makers.

The next illustration illustrates different key skeletons that are possible to manufacture.

Chapter 16: Pin Tumbler & Wafer

The tools needed to open both types of locks are the same which is why they are considered in conjunction.

But, contrary to common opinion, there aren't any key skeletons that can allow you to open the lock like in the films. It the key is more dependent on skills and training.

Hook Picks

This is for the purpose of "pure picking" as described in the section on techniques.

What is required in this case is to know the basics of what they are, and be aware that they are available in different sizes.

Rakes

Rakes come in a wide range of forms and sizes. Below, you can see a few of the most popular ones.

Turning Tools/Tension Wrench

Bypass Pick

It can be constructed by grinding a saw blade into a tapered shape like the one shown below.

Lever

Lifter Picks

The dimensions of this lock will be decided by the lever lock that is to be grabbed.

Turning Tool/Tension Wrench

Although it shares similar names to those is used to make wafer and pin locks, it is very distinct in its construction. In terms of form as well as the quality of the steel used. The reasons behind this will be covered in the section on methods.

Combination Brief Case

Combination Probe

This kind of pick doesn't need the same strength as the similarly-sized bypass picks used in pin tumbler locks, but should be very thin.

The probe serves only the goal of opening the brief case combination locks.

The probe I designed to use in this experiment was constructed out of a gauge for a feeling. It was in particular

a number 12

Constructing Picks

While they are not expensive to purchase, they can become a bit difficult to locate the right outlets that offer them.

It is not an issue since the proper choices can be built yourself with just a bit of time and effort.

For making an effective pick, it's an absolute requirement to possess a grinder as grinding tools cannot shape the necessary metal to produce last a long-lasting and durable pick.

That brings us to a crucial issue i.e. What metal is best to use and how can it be sourced? For a metal to be useful, it should meet two primary requirements. It should be sturdy as well as light, (to get past any fancy keyhole that is between the user and device).

This kind of metal is easily located in hacksaw blades. They are able to be marked with shapes of picks with the making use of a permanent pen and then ground precisely to form the desired shape. Metal is very useful and is able for the construction of hook picks, rakes lever locks, bypass picks and lifter pick.

Sets of gauges for feelers, are available at hardware or automotive stores, are also made of metals that are able to be used.

While some can only be used for shims, they are also able to be used as probes or picks (especially combined probes) according to their strength and the thickness.

The material used to make turning tools, both for the lever and pin tumbler can differ. A turning tool is used for opening the lid of a pin tumbler secure any metal that is bent in the above-depicted shape, i.e, the straight easy turning tool that is straight forward A without becoming a stale shape, is enough.

The tool for turning the lever lock is made from the most sturdy and rigid steel. It ought to be made of a material that, once it is in the desired form, it will not bend. it can generate a powerful turn force.

Warded

The process of opening padlocks was covered in the section on tools. The method by that these locks are unlocked is via a the skeleton key. The only thing left is to test each key you have included in the set, no matter if it was purchased or made by you, after inserting the key into the lock in as much as is possible. If there is no luck in unlocking the lock, take your key away from the lock a little and then turn the key once more.

In accordance with the amount of keys that you have you will be able to unlock a variety of locks at a minimum effort, by attempting every key in this manner.

Pin tumbler, and Wafer

Pure Picking

This method of picking demands the use of more skills, patience and experience than the other technique of raking, but when you master it, it is a highly beneficial method of achieving.

This way of opening may be applied to both the pin tumbler as well as the wafer lock, and requires using hook picks.

The first thing to do is insert the proper hook in the lock to ensure that it's through the lock.

The tool that turns is installed in the keyway with the tool is gently turned. It is only a slight pressurization is required, otherwise the pins could bind, i.e. they would jam into the lock.

By pressing the rotating tool, a slight pushing motion is applied to the tool to gradually elevate the pin to the top. It is important to be mentioned is to lift all pins that are on the top of the upper chamber inside the locking. Thus, the pins at the bottom are to be permitted to drop back to the lower casing after the pick is moved towards the pin that is next. The lower pin is not to be elevated above the shear lines.

While lifting the pair of driver pins, and lower pins, at the point where the highest point of the lower pin is the shear line, only a brief click is expected and the pin loses any springiness.

After this has been felt, slide the pick downwards and then out toward the back of the lock, so that contact with the pin next will be achieved. Similar prying motions and sensitivity is required. Keep going until all pins are raised above the shear line, at which point the lock is finally ready to yield.

In the course of this process, only one gentle turn will be applied.

Raking

If you can master this technique correctly, could be the fastest method of opening the pin tumbler or wafer lock.

The idea behind this method is to cause the pins to move, making them bounce around on the line of shear. It will result in several of the best drivers to come off the plug while others will remain to the plug. This makes the pins moved in an unplanned manner which means that they are not a perfect match. With different shapes of rakes, the lift pattern is different and the chance of chance of success is higher.

Raking can also affect the wafer locks. Ragging makes the wafers move up and down, as well as to determine the proper locations that allow the cylinder to rotate.

The rake must be positioned on the rear on the locking. The tool for turning is in the keyway however there is no pressure placed on the tool. This is the only time that the tool is released from the lock, that the tension, or a soft tension is pressed.

Every rake needs to be used minimum 15 times before you find a new one that works.

Bypassing

This technique can be utilized with padlocks, as well as filing cabinets, which are locked by a pin that protrudes from an upper portion or the bottom.

The bypass pick that is shown in the section Tools will be utilized. This method is easy and efficient as it doesn't require the skills required to use the two above methods. The only thing necessary is a knowledge of the purpose for which a bypass pick can be used for, and the diagram below should be able to demonstrate.

Shimming is a method to unlock padlocks secured with a pin tumbler. This technique also prevents you from having pick the lock. This is done by simply attacking the area of the lock that locks the shackle.

The following diagram demonstrates how the shim works and opens the shackle.

Lever

This kind of lock is widely used throughout the UK for door locks as well as padlocks.

For opening this type of lock, the pick for lifting and turning tool mentioned in the section on tools are necessary.

The turning tool exerts continuous pressure to the bolt that locks during the raising of levers.

The lifting tool lifts every lever, and when it has been raised to the proper height, it will remain in position through the force of the bolt, generated by the pressure that is created by the force of a turning tool. Thus, a strong turning tool is necessary since the springs of the levers can't be overridden, thus bringing each lever back to its initial position after the pick for lifting is taken away.

The pick for the lifter can be set to the rear of the lock, lifting each lever individually but I like lifting the lever first because it is more difficult to lift up initially, allowing the bolt to put more force on the other levers once they have been raised.

When a lever has been elevated to the proper height, there will be a small tension in the bolt since there is just one lever to stop the slide. The lever which has been elevated should be easier to move because the surface of the bolt won't be in contact with the lever as it is within it's gate.

You can move on to the next lever, whether it is that next lever on the line, or the one that is the most difficult to shift. The next time, less pressure will be applied to the tension wrench. However, make sure that you don't let the first lever to revert to its initial location. The second lever(s) may be pulled using the same method until the bolt is through the entire length and then the lock can be opened.

Chapter 17: Padlocks

Dial

There are many padlocks that use an arrangement in the shape of a dial, as seen in the photo below.

The method by which this locks function has been covered in the article of mechanisms, so once you have an understanding of how the lock can be opened will be discussed.

It is important to understand that doing is turning the dial in the proper sequence is to set all of the gates into the same location which allows that the bolt slide in it, allowing the shackle to raise it up.

For opening this lock the first step to do is put the shackle with pressure. It is accomplished by putting the lock with your less strong hand, and then placing your finger underneath the shackle, and pushing it up. The result is that you make the bolt holding the shackle in place to move up. This will cause the part that is locked to be able to move into the space created by gates to be pushed against the wheels, which causes friction. In theoretical terms, when this locking element gets to the gates, the dial is likely to thump. It will it will then soften. As a result of other wheels pressing down on the locking component and limiting the motion of the locking bolt, the thump and the lack of friction could be diminished.

That's why it's essential to pay attention and the sensations you feel once the gates have been reached. Additionally, it may be helpful placing the lock in front of your ear as you turn the dial so that you can detect more clearly the time where the thump takes place.

Once the initial number has been attained, the dial needs to be rotated in the reverse direction for by one full revolution. The identical procedure is followed to detect the number two.

The third number can be discovered easily the number is reached following the change of direction on the dial after the second time the shackle will into open. This will make the dial, upon initially turning to stop and make a click that is quite loud, and cannot be mistaken for the number that was first rung.

Dial: With Push Closed Clasp

While these locks are able to be opened the same manner as described in the previous paragraph, due to their capacity to squeeze shut, they are accessible to a technique that eliminates the requirement for the sensitivity process mentioned earlier. This allows them to be opened faster and without much effort.

The only way they are opened is through shmming. Shimming is the process of inserting a shim down to the outside of the shackle, causing it to pull the locking bolt inwards.

In the case of the lock that is not snap-closed, after the dial is moved in the right order and the shackle has been in the open position, if it is turned while the shackle in an locked position, then the lock wouldn't be able to be locked since the bolt will not be able to be able to spring back.

This is the point the area where the snap-closed padlock differs from the snap closed, since when the dial has been moved with the shackle removed of the lock, the lock could be locked once more because the bolt can spring into place when the shackle is placed in the lock.

Below is a diagram that illustrates the differences between the locking bolts used in snap-closed lock and snap-closed locks.

A lot of combination dial locks feature circular bodies and permit ease of access to the bolt that is spring loaded.

A different aspect should be considered in relation to the padlock dial. The reason is that after one has put the shackle into place, they often do not turn the dial in enough so that it alters the direction of all the locks' wheels. This is why a lock that is this kind can typically open quickly simply turning the dial counterclockwise slow. The reason for this is that most users are left-handed which means that they will turn the dial when they lock it clockwise. Since they can only turn about half of a revolution, the only wheel to shift will be the top wheel and will not affect the remaining locations for the gates. Thus, by turning the dial again in the reverse direction, it will replace the gate to the correct position that allows the bolt to rotate and the lock to unlock.

Push Button

The padlock of this kind is fairly modern. A good illustration of this could be found below.

It can be opened this manner.

By applying tension to the knob at the top of the lock, gently press the button to the left side upwards. They will be identified by numbers 1-5.

All numbers include gates that permit a grid to move. This slide action happens when the button located at the base is released and the bolt is moved from the shackle. But, the buttons limit the sliding action, thus keeping the shackle.

A correct combination allows the inside grid to move because the gates or notches that are in the button's lugs will be above the buttons that those on buttons that don't belong to the set. Thus, when entering the correct combination, what happens is that all gates are aligned, which allows that the grid's position to change, and the bolt to break from the shackle.

In the course of picking this kind of lock after the buttons have been moved downwards and tension is applied to the button's bottom, it is likely that a few of these buttons are not lower as far as they can be. This could be because they have gates below them that aren't included in the lock combination.

Thus, when you put pressure onto the slide when those were raised, it resulted in the grid being forced to go into gates a little, thus limiting the slide's movement down. The next step is lift the numbers that did not fall completely into the lock since only half of the code was found. You just need to eliminate the numbers that don't belong to of the sequence.

The next thing to do is press down without tension on the next column of numbers i.e. 6-0. Then, by applying pressure to the slide button, all you need to do is gentle pushing of the buttons up one after one. Because the buttons that form included in the combination are already alignment with the grid, and the consequence when you apply pressure on the slide can limit the movement of these buttons upwards. But the numbers not forming part of the combo however they are able to move up. The only thing left for you to do is ensure that all buttons that make up the combination have been fully pressed as well as that the numbers that are not part of the combo are removed from the lock. The lock must now give.

Disk

The padlock type can be observed in the picture below.

The key to unlocking this lock like the majority of combination locks, is applying pressure.

The pressure is applied to the shackle, which could result in creating one of the disks be rigid and difficult to turn. The disk that is first worked on. It is all that is needed is to rotate the disk while retaining the tension on the shackle till the tension has been released. This is the time when the portion of the shackle that was blocked from advancing across the disk will now be able to be able to pass through, as the gate is at the same position.

The correct information of the disk you have worked on will result in tension that can be transferred to another disk. The right number for this disk is obtainable using the same method like you did before.

Because these kinds of locks are only made up of three disks, the only thing you have for you to do is turn the last disk till the lock is snapped open by the force of your pushing the lock's shackle.

Bicycle Chain

It could appear in either of the images as shown below.

The keys can be removed similar to the way like the padlock on a disk as described above.

Certain important aspects are to be considered. Tension is required to allow to identify exactly where the gates are located. Because the gates represent points on the disks that there is no metal and the peg that is corresponding to the shackle won't create tension and becomes loose.

But, because of the additional disks that are taking on the tension after the initial number is identified, it could frequently be hard to perceive. It is here that practice can pay off since this distinctness will be easily discernible.

Brief Case

This kind of lock is able to very easily be opened by the aid of a specifically made tool. This tool was discussed in the section on tools which is why reference is required.

The workings of this kind of lock needs to be thoroughly comprehended in order to successfully open it. Thus, one should look back at the mechanics section, where the lock was described. Like all locks it is the best method to know the mechanism of a lock is to unlock it your self, which can't be overemphasized enough.

If the inside operation of this lock is scrutinized, you will see that at the exact point you can find the correct number located, there is a tiny notch found. That is the notch that the probe, also known as a feeler probe is trying to locate. It is also a lot smaller than the other parts of the disk. Therefore, the same can be felt. correctly. The best place to place the probe. The probe should be placed on the right side of the dial closest to the button. It is also closest to the havep. It is best to place it on the sides of the disk till it makes contact by the ring made of plastic that the disk sits upon. The plastic ring turns along with the metal ring thanks to projections that are projected onto it in the form of a star. But, inside this rings is a flat section that is that is located directly adjacent to the number in the concatenation. That is the thing that the probe tool will be looking for as it goes down the inside of each disk.

Chapter 18: A Quick Background Of Locks And Lock Picking

Ever since humans began gathering items which were meant to be used only by themselves and not shared with anyone else there have been people who have a goal of stealing these items from their owners which has led to the necessity of keep these objects safe from thieves.

Prior to locks being invented, there was another kinds of locking mechanism that were in use throughout the centuries, twine, ropes and cords were utilized in order to " lock" doors and other objects in place, much as locks do nowadays. There were knots that were intricately designed for this purpose creating the knotted rope as an iconic symbol of security. As an illustration, there was the Gordian Knot, a knot that was which was so intricate that the legend said only the one who was bound to be the conqueror of Asia could pull it loose, knotted by Gordius King of Phrygia which secured the rope to the shaft on his horse.

If Alexander was the Great as a conqueror, failed to unravel the Gordian knot, he cut the knot quickly with his sword, making it among the earliest known actions of locking picking.

The first mechanical locks were constructed from wood. Documents show they were being used for over 4,000 years in Egypt.

The very first wooden lock was found in Persia in the form of Khorsabad within the security gate inside Sargon II's palace. Sargon II, who ruled between 705 and 722 BC.

Khorsabad, Persia In appearance and function, this lock is identical to the timber cane-tumble lock.

The pegs that are located at the end of the key are the bars, or tumblers that are within the bolt. After being inserted, the pegs raised the tumblers, so that the bolt can be pulled back so that the gate or door was able to be opened. This lock was the precursor to modern lock with pins tumblers.

It wasn't until 870-900 that the first locks made of all metal were designed in England and were just simple locks made from iron, with obstructions that were placed over the keyholes to stop tampering. they locks were forerunners of modern Warded Locks as well as inspired by a concept first developed through the Romans who designed obstructions in order to "ward off" the entry or making of a incorrect key.

Lock Picking turned into a cult art in the 18th century, and lock makers needed to come up with more complex locking mechanisms in order to limit the activities of potential be thieves. They developed keys with interchangeable bits and locks that had curtains closed around keyholes, alarms that worked with the actions of bolts and puzzle padlocks (predecessors to locking mechanisms that combine).

In America between 1774 to 1920 American lock makers had patented more than 3000 different locking devices One of those patents was a lock invented by Linus Yale, who was a reworking of an older Egyptian pin-tumbler design which used a revolving cylindrical.

The 1920's were the time when Walter Schlage advanced the concept of cylindrical pin-tumbler locks installing a lock push button mechanism inside the knobs.

Chapter 19: Different Locks And Mechanisms

The Warded Lock:

The warded lock is among of the oldest locks that is still used today. It is believed to be the product of China before spreading to Europe in the middle ages.

For locks with basic warded locks an obstruction would stop the movement of a keys that are not specifically designed for the lock. The locks could be equipped with just one basic ward, or a number of wards that are complex with protrusions and bends However, the fundamental principle is identical, except that if the shape of the key is similar to those of the locks' wards and it hits the obstruction, and not rotate at all.

Once a valid key has been put into the lock it will break through the wards, and then rotate around the central post. After that, it will impact the lever, which will trigger the lock or sliding bolt to let the lock open.

The key gets into through the keyhole. When the key is fully in through the hole, the end of the key can be inserted into a post that is cylindrical inside the lock. It provides a pivot point that the key may rotate.

The notches on the key are aligned with the obstacles or the wards, allowing the key to freely rotate, so the key can trigger an lever or a sliding bolt to unlock the lock.

The pin tumbler Lock

Pin tumbler locks are the lock the most frequently used in commercial and residential cylinder lock.

The pin tumbler lock, the exterior casing is fitted with a circular hole inside where the plug is stored for opening the door, the pin has to rotate within the hole.

It has an opening on one side called the keyway that lets the key in into it. At the opposite side, it could be equipped with an lever or cam that triggers a mechanism that retracts the bolt to let the lock open. There are a series of holes set vertically within the plug, which are filled with key pins with various sizes, and there could be anywhere from five to six holes that contain pins, which are then rounded in order to allow the key to be easily slipped over them.

Over each pin, there is an identical set of driver pins with spring loaded. The casing's outer part has a number of vertical shafts that hold the pins that are spring loaded.

The simplest locks usually have just one driver pin per key pin. However, locks with multi-keyed access, for example, a collection of locks that have an master key may contain additional driver pins, referred to as spacer pins.

After the plug and its outer assembly is put together in this way, the pins will be pushed downwards into the plug through the springs. The location between the cylinder and the plug join is referred to as Shear Point. If the right key is placed in the lock the pins will raise, causing them to be aligned precisely at the point of shear. The plug will then be able to turn to open the lock.

If the key isn't inside the lock, or a key is incorrectly inserted inside the keyway pins are not aligned to the shear points, which hinders the plug from turning.

Locks with two keys that allow it to be opened as master keys have two shear points. The first set is the same as all other locks within the set while another set of shear points are distinct to this lock.

The Padlock:

Padlocks were first introduced in times to Greeks, Romans, Egyptians as well as the Chinese It was initially utilized as a travel lock to secure goods from theft on trade routes that were ancient and which were the hub of commerce. they were not all that big, and some had huge dimensions They were constructed of copper, iron or brass and had a sturdy construction.

The shackle usually appears like an "U", round or with a square cross-section. It usually can be swung away from or slip off the padlock body when it is in an unlocked state.

The earlier padlocks were fitted with locking mechanisms integrated into them and their designs was not able to be disassembled and used moving disks or lever tumblers that let a small portion of the bolt which secures the shackle is inserted into the tumblers once a proper key is turned to the lock.

Modern modular locking systems do not utilize the tumblers in a direct way for locking the shackle, they incorporate a plug into the cylinder, which when connected to the key that is correctly inserted, turns and lets a dog to retract away from the cutting notches into the shackle.

Padlocks that have locks that have modular mechanisms are able to be removed to alter the tumblers, or for servicing the lock. They typically utilize pin, wafer and disk tumblers. They can also be automated and self-locking without require a key for locking the padlock.

Chapter 20: Tools And Equipment Of The Locksmith

The Tension or Torque Wrench:

The tension, or Torque Wrench is an "L" shaped tool used to pick locks using tension or pressure on the internal cylinder of the lock in order to secure any pins that are picked on the lock while other pins are moved and when all the pins are chosen, the tool is used move the cylinder inside to open the lock just like keys.

Although it is not a tool, this one offers torsion, not tension. it is a tool that stretches a thing while torsion twists it.

Certain torsion wrenches are referred to as "Feather Touch" and are connected to a spring by the angle of the "L" which helps the user to maintain a an unstoppable tension.

Forked Torsion wrench is similar to the twisters that are used in vehicles. They allow the user the ability to apply tension to the sides and the top of the lock. It typically used in dual-sided wafer locks.

A few high tech tools for torsion are placed over the lock, allowing users to view an indication of the level of pressure being applied. This assists in sensing when a lock is been positioned.

The Torsion tool is as crucial as lock picks. It is impossible to choose a pin/tumbler wafer lock, without even by using an instrument for picking.

The Half- Diamond Pick:

The most fundamental and widely used picks is for picking pins by hand however it could also be utilized for raking, and to pick disk and wafer locks.

It's similar to the half-diamond, however it is a hook-tip instead of a half-diamond form It is also known as the feeler pick. It does not have a raking function however it can be used to determine how each pin is that is raised up until it reaches that shear line.

Picks like the snake-shaped picks are specifically designed specifically to "rake" pins by rapidly shifting the pick through each pin, so that they bounce off the pins to their shear lines.

This is the simplest method and usually works with less expensive locks. After the pins have been released, they bounce around the shear line. the use of a skilled Torsion wrenches is the most efficient method to select locks.

Warded Lock Picks:

The warded pick is also called a skeleton key, is utilized to open warded locks. They can be made to fit an overall key shape in order that allows internal manipulations Additionally, these picks may be utilized in order to "rip" the lock by setting the pick in the rear of the lock, and then taking it away using a quick cutting motion.

The Pick Gun:

It is the Pick Gun is used by pulling the trigger. It works on the same principles that Newton's Cradle does, which is to transmit energy upwards to the lower pins, which relays it to the top pins, which causes these pins to leap at the same time the pick gun must always be utilized in conjunction with a wrench torsion and all that is required to unlock the lock is knowing the exact timing for the snap.

Additionally, there are electric pick guns that can be operated can be operated by pressing one button causes the gun's pick to shake together with the wrench to be employed causes the pins to be move to herar lines.

Chapter 21: Make Your Own Lock Picks As Well As Tension Wrenches

Materials and tools required to create your tools and picks

It is recommended to have:

1. Flat Steel Strips.

2. Electrical Tape.

3. Metal Shears.

6. Bench Vise (optional)

7. Bench Grinder (optional) 8. Rubber Cement or Glue 4. An assortment of Small Metal Files. 9. Needle nose pliers 5. Small Hole Rubber Tubing

Metal Sheers, small files, the rubber cement the needle nose pliers as well as Electrical Tape are available inexpensively at the local hardware store. A bench vise as well as a grinder for bench use can cost a lot If you own them, utilize them. If not, go with the more affordable tables for filing, and utilize the small file. If you want the flat steel strips you could go to your nearest dollar shop and buy the Folding Hamper as pictured below at just one dollar. Then, you can remove the rods made of flat steel which hold it in place and slice it using the metal shears in 6 inch strips.

Pop Up Hamper Open Hamper Take out Flat Steel Rods

6 inches

Slice rod into 6-inch Strips. One pop up hammer is enough flat steel strips that you can make many sets of picks as well as tension wrenches.

Making the Tension Wrenches:

To create a straightforward "L" shaped tension wrench it is as easy as taking one of the 6-inch steel sheets and then form it to the "L" shape with the needle nose pliers shown below.

Simple Double-ended Tension Wrench.

In order to make the Feather Finger Tension wrench, you have to bend the strip of steel at the top of the "L" shape to form a spring, as shown below.

Masking the Half- Diamond Pick:

To create the half-diamond, make a half-diamond pick, place a flat strip of steel on the bench vice or make use of your pliers secure the strip.

Filing on Vice

Filing on Table

The tip that is filed should appear similar to the one on this piece of fruit.

To make the handle of the pick, you need to cut 3 inches from the tiny hole rubber tubing. Then, put on the electric tape at the handle portion of the instrument you've just constructed.

Cut 3 inches of tubing to cover the handle in tape After that, cover the taped portion with glue or rubber cement, and then place the 3 inch tube on top of the tape and glue.

Pushing the Tube

Making the Hook Pick:

The tube is 3 inches deep into the handle

Use the same method you did to make the half-diamond selection, but the result should appear similar to those shown below.

Hook Tip

How to make the Snake Rake pick:

Repeat the process, however, outcomes should be similar to this:

Snake Rake Tip

Another pick that is not often used which is the rounded Rake Pick.

Round Rake Pick Here are all of the finalized wrenches and picks.

To create warded lockpicks it is necessary to cut these forms from a thick sheets of iron.

Another device that can be made from steel that is heavy They are known as keys for Automotive Test-Out.

The steps to make use of those keys within the following chapter.

Note A note: Creating the tools illustrated with the use of hand files could be an arduous task you will need patience and some elbow grease to get the desired shape for every tool.

The bench grinder is a great tool to speed up the process and help make the task easier however, they can be costly. costing between $100.00 to $1000.

If you own the bench grinder, or have it available from someone, try it. If not, take your time and if your first attempt doesn't come out correctly, you can try it again. The pop-up hamper provided enough steel pieces which allow you to fail and have the materials.

Bench Grinder

Chapter 22: Different Methods For Unlocking Locked Doors

Selecting the pin tumbler lock:

The majority of pin tumbler locks are fitted with up to five pins. it includes all padlocks not of locked with a combination, such as deadbolts, doorknob locks as well as automobiles.

Pin tumbler locks are one of the most commonly used locks can be found, and they are commonly used in homes school, workplaces, business premises as well as other locations. The pin tumbler lock offers the greatest security at a reasonable price, but as they're priced affordable, they're easy to choose.

Pick and tension wrench work together to select the lock. To select the pin tumbler lock, you simply need to place the pins in the shear points one after one. Once one pin has reached the shear point, when you press it using your pick and apply tension using the torsion wrench, the lock rotates only a little, enough to allow it to press the pin that drives it between the shaft and the plug, pressing it in such a way that, once you remove your finger it remains within the shaft but is released from the plug as long as you hold the wrench's tension continuously. Repeat this process for every pin, and the plug will turn in a way that the driving pins remain in the shaft and the key pins fall to the lowest place in the plug when the pick has been removed. and then release the tension slowly and rotate the torsion wrench to open the doors.

The Raking Method:

Raking is the most efficient and fast way to open locks.

Making the pins

Insert the Snake Rake Pick all the up to the rear of the plug. While applying tension using the wrench and rake the pins by bending them in a downward direction. Repeat the process till all of the pins on top are raised and all the important pins fall until they are at the bottom of the plug. Slowly let the tension go and then turn the wrench until it opens the door.

It is important to note that there two aspects which are crucial in order to choose the lock.

1. Be sure to check the position of the pins prior to you decide to choose the lock. Usually, the pins are in the upper portion of the plug. Therefore, the lock will be placed at the top of the plug and your tension wrench will be at below the top of the socket, but occasionally due to some reason, locks are put in upside-down and this alters the manner you have to utilize your tools. Now you have to insert the tool

at the top of the plug with the tension wrench at the top.

2. It is essential to understand how to rotate the tension wrench to unblock the lock when you've selected it. making the wrench turn incorrectly won't unlock the lock, but it'll make the pins reset, which means you have to select the lock again, unless you employ an instrument that is specifically designed for this purpose, referred to as an a plug spinner.

The plug spinner is springs configured to spin in the direction you want it to spin. It does this so quickly, so that it is able to bypass the shear line and unlock the lock.

A lock that is normally fitted can be opened when the bolt is rotated in the opposite direction to the jam on the door. Doing this, the bolt will be pulled back away from the plate on the jam.

Once a lock has been installed, the Upside Down the lock will be opened after the plug has been turned toward the door jam. By doing this, it will remove the bolt off the door's plate Jam.

The Feel Method:

The method of feeling is more difficult than raking because it takes a lot of patience experience each pin.

Beginning with the first pin then push it higher by applying light pressure using the tension wrench. Remember to use the wrench to exert pressure to the point that the lock should open once the driving pin is stuck between the shaft and the plug and you'll feel the plug turns in a slight manner. In order to prove you've got that pin in the proper position, let go of the tension from the torsion wrench. You are likely to hear a click which signifies that the pin was chosen right. Pick it up again, then repeat for each pin until the plug is turned and the lock unlocks.

The door can be opened using the credit card

A few doors can be unlocked making use of credit card plastic card. We would not suggest the use of a credit card that is valid to open doors unless it is an emergency situation, as the card could be damaged during the process. Instead, you should use an old card, or similar slim plastic card with similar shape.

Doors that are open using credit cards should not have deadbolts since this method is not applicable to these locks, but only for the knob-type door lock.

Credit card methods work with door knob locks however is not applicable to deadbolt locks.

The first step is to turn the knob on your door to determine whether the door is dead bolted or was locked with the bolt of the door knob at the exit, in the event that it was secured by the knob, the door will not move. There is a chance that the door could still be locked however, you'll need to get the knob locked.

Check the Door

Then, take the card and take it and slide it to the bottom of the door until that the card is in contact with the bolt of lock.

Place the card side of the door between the jam and slide it to the left until it touches the bolt of lock.

You can then wiggle your card in downward direction, pressing and pulling on the knob on the door to move it between locks bolts and door frame.

Move the card between the bolt of lock as well as the door frame.

When you've got your card in within the lock between it and door frame, you can bend the ends of the card to the frame so that you can push the bolt into the lock to pull it out and push to open the door.

This technique works great for doors that are open to the outside and doors that open outwards, the procedure differs somewhat due to the way that the door bolt is reversed.

I've created a set of tools that can unlock both doors both ways, inwards and outwards. it is possible to make these tools at home using very cheap tools and materials.

The tool can be used to open upward doors using the credit card method, however I've utilized a less expensive spatula, and then cut it in order to place it in the place where the bolt for locking is and push into the tool to unlock the door.

Tool for opening doors in the outward direction The other tool helps in opening doors inwards This tool works as a credit card, by placing the tool on the bolt of lock and twisting the tool as you pull and pushing.

Tool for Inward door opening

This tool is able to open all kinds of doors. It has two hack saw blades which when combined will secure onto the bolt of lock and unlock the door through pushing or pulling.

Doors that can be opened by both kinds of doors.

Auto Jigglers and try the keys:

Like we promised in the first chapter, we'll now show the use of auto Jigglers or to test out keys, as they are known occasionally to open doors in cars.

These keys are a collection of lockpicks that are designed to assist in opening doors on cars. They can be used on vehicles that were manufactured between 1999 and.

In order to make the right choice, it is essential to find a tool which most likely looks like the genuine car key However, as most of the times you do not have keys, you need to "Try-Out" all of the instruments until you locate the one that is working which is why the name "Try-Out" was chosen for these keys.

The directions provided by the company state that you need to place the tool between your thumb and forefinger, and apply pressure either counter-clockwise or clockwise, while moving the tool into as well out using an raking motion. However, when I the first time I tried this method, it was somewhat awkward, so I came up with my own way of doing it making use of the Forked Torsion wrench to apply the tension, while paying attention to the raking movement in and out from the device.

In order to speed up the opening procedure, you might want to pair the process earlier with a slight motion to boost the chance of the success.

Here you go everything you've always had wanted to know about picking locks and were hesitant to ask.

We wish you the best of luck in using the knowledge you have acquired to assist people in times in need. There is no more harrowing feeling than being trapped in your own vehicle or home.

www.ingramcontent.com/pod-product-compliance
Lightning Source LLC
Chambersburg PA
CBHW071444080526
44587CB00014B/1978